Meditation & the Martial Arts

Studies in Religion & Culture

Frank Burch Brown
Gary L. Ebersole
Edith Wyschogrod

EDITORS

Meditation & the Martial Arts

Michael L. Raposa

University of Virginia Press
Charlottesville and London

University of Virginia Press

© 2003 by the Rector and Visitors of the University of Virginia

All rights reserved

Printed in the United States of America on acid-free paper

First published 2003

1 3 5 7 9 8 6 4 2

Library of Congress Cataloging-in-Publication Data

Raposa, Michael L.

   Meditation and the martial arts / Michael L. Raposa.

      p. cm. — (Studies in religion and culture)

   Includes bibliographical references and index.

   ISBN 0-8139-2238-0 (cloth : alk. paper)

   1. Martial arts—Psychological aspects. 2. Meditation.

I. Title. II. Studies in religion and culture (Charlottesville, Va.)

   GV1102.7.P75R36 2003

   796.8'01'9—dc21

2003007965

For my children,
Daniel, Elizabeth, and Rosemary,

And for Joseph H. Brehm,
in memoriam

Contents

Preface

Philosophers of religion have devoted considerable energy to the analysis of religious beliefs and doctrines, as well as to the evaluation of descriptive accounts of religious experience. Religious *practices*, however, have received far less attention. What religious folk think and feel has been deemed important, but what they *do* has attracted comparatively little philosophical interest.

I have now begun to direct more of my own attention, both as a teacher and a scholar, to the philosophical task of exploring the significance of certain religious practices. Since 1995, I have regularly taught an introductory course entitled "Spiritual Exercises East and West." Its subject matter consists of disciplines drawn from a variety of religious traditions, ranging from the practice of yoga and certain martial arts to the spiritual exercises of Saint Ignatius of Loyola. The course was designed with multiple objectives. It was intended, first, to supply a historical and cultural perspective on these practices. At the same time, I have struggled to develop a fresh philosophical account of the nature and meaning of spiritual discipline and to offer some evaluation of the contemporary relevance of such exercises. What happens, for example, when modern practitioners disengage these disciplines from their original religious context, pursuing them primarily for purposes of health or even recreation? Can the original religious purpose of these exercises be articulated in a contemporary idiom, perhaps defended and pursued?

In my *Boredom and the Religious Imagination*, published in 1999, I explored the problem of boredom and concomitant distractions as they afflict practitioners engaged in various spiritual exercises (prayer, meditation, ritual and liturgical devotions, etc.). In the attempt to resist these distractions, the religious devotee is sometimes portrayed as being engaged in a form of "spiritual combat," typically with an enemy who is frighteningly real. Also in 1999, I published an article in the *American Journal of Theology and Philosophy* entitled "Pragmatism, Budō, and the *Spiritual Exercises:* The Moral Equivalent of War"; the following year, my essay "Self-Control" was published in the same journal. Those articles were modified versions of some of the draft material for this book.

Since 1990, I have been engaged in the study of several martial arts: aikidō (a Japanese discipline with roots in traditional Shintō and in Buddhism) and the Chinese Daoist arts of taijiquan and baguazhang. I have also trained more briefly in tang soo do (a Korean martial art) and iaidō (the highly ritualistic Japanese sword-drawing art). My study has included reading and scholarly investigation, but I have also been fortunate to encounter outstanding teachers of these martial arts, with whom I have been able to enjoy regular practice. After more than a dozen years of training, my level of skill in these disciplines remains rudimentary. Nonetheless, the ongoing practice has added to these philosophical meditations a certain existential dimension.

I am greatly indebted to my teachers in the martial arts, not only for their superb instruction but also for the patience and kindness displayed toward a sincere but ungifted, middle-aged student. With deep gratitude and respect, I acknowledge Sensei Minh Nguyen, Sensei Ninh Le (aikidō), Sifu William Newman, Sifu Robert Fischer (taiji and bagua), Sabom John Gallagher (tang soo do), and Sensei Shuji Matsushita (iaidō).

This study is the sort of project that never becomes more than the germ of an idea without the support of friends and colleagues at the earliest stages. In this regard, I am especially grateful to Cathie Brettschneider for her patience as well as her confidence and to Norman Girardot, Robert Neville, and Carol Zaleski for their insight and encouragement. I am indebted in a similar fashion to all of my colleagues in the Religion Studies

Department at Lehigh University (especially Ben Wright, who graciously offered his expertise and advice whenever I came knocking at his door), as well as to my friends in the Lehigh Valley Aikikai (in particular, Andrew Grochowski, a true scholar of budō). Alan Heverly kindly agreed to read the completed manuscript, supplying valuable feedback. And David Pankenier was generous with his expertise concerning the correct usage and spelling of certain Chinese and Japanese terms.

Courage, loyalty, and love are all keys to victory in the "spiritual combat." No one has taught me more about these qualities than my wife, Mary Ellen. My gratitude for her wisdom, patience, support, and editor's insight is, like the Dao itself, too great to be spoken.

One of the masterpieces of martial spirituality is a short treatise from seventeenth-century Japan entitled "The Clear Sound of Jewels." In appreciation for their having filled my house and heart with a delightful sound, I dedicate this book to Daniel, Elizabeth, and Rosemary, the three precious jewels of my life.

This work is also dedicated to my father-in-law, Joseph Brehm, in memory of a life shaped by a tremendous spirit of love.

Meditation & the Martial Arts

Introduction

Early in the seventeenth century, the Japanese Zen Buddhist monk Takuan Sōhō wrote a long letter to Yagyu Munenori, his friend and a martial artist of some renown. In it, he recommended cultivation of the state of *mushin* ("no-mind") as being most conducive to success in combat. "Completely oblivious to the hand that wields the sword, one strikes and cuts his opponent down. He does not put his mind in his adversary. The opponent is Emptiness. I am Emptiness. The hand that holds the sword, the sword itself, is Emptiness. Understand this, but do not let your mind be taken by Emptiness. . . . For the striking sword, there is no mind. For myself, who is about to be struck, there is no mind."[1]

In a letter written many centuries earlier, Saint Paul had offered his advice to the members of the Christian community at Ephesus regarding their preparation for engagement in a different form of combat.[2] He counseled each of them to "take up the whole armor of God, so that you may be able to withstand in the evil day, and having done everything, to stand firm. Stand therefore, and fasten the belt of truth around your waist, and put on the breastplate of righteousness. As shoes for your feet put on whatever will make you ready to proclaim the gospel of peace. With all of these, take the shield of faith, with which you will be able to quench all the flaming arrows of the evil one. Take the helmet of salvation, and the sword of the Spirit, which is the word of God."[3]

The contents of these letters are strikingly dissimilar; the writers themselves were far removed from one another in place and in history, representing two quite distinctive religious perspectives and addressing themselves to readers with very different beliefs and concerns. Yet the juxtaposition of these two passages establishes several interesting points of contact. Both writers directed their advice to readers who had to be prepared for the eventuality of combat, the possible encounter with a dangerous enemy. And both Takuan and Paul drew upon the resources supplied by the spiritual traditions of their respective religious communities in order to formulate their prescriptions for success in battle.

This book is about the relationship between meditation and the martial arts. That relationship is a complex one, and multifaceted. Meditation is one of the practices in which martial artists engage in order to prepare for combat. At the same time, the physical exercises that constitute much of the discipline of the martial arts can themselves be conceived as meditative practices, forms of "moving meditation," so to speak. (This is the case, most especially, with Japanese aikidō, iaidō, and kyudō and the Chinese arts identified as "internal.") Finally, there is a sense in which meditation itself can be conceived as a form of combat. A variety of spiritual disciplines not classified as "martial arts" make heavy use of martial images and categories as a part of their self-description (examples are abundant, a prime one being Ignatius of Loyola's spiritual exercises). Here the practice of prayer, meditation, or ritual devotion is itself regarded as being a martial activity. What is the nature of the conflict here and who is the enemy? Does the use of these martial categories imply that we are speaking in such an instance (as William James did) of something like the "moral [or spiritual] equivalent of war"?

I propose some possible answers to these questions. My interest is both in the martial arts conceived as meditative practices and in meditation conceived as a martial discipline. I am convinced that these are not two separate concerns, but rather two different ways of looking at the same thing. In order to pursue this topic, it is necessary for me to consider some concrete examples of arts identified both as martial and as meditative. It is not my primary purpose to narrate the complex history of these arts or to produce a comprehensive survey of martial disciplines and of their religious origins and characteristics.[4] Nor is this a practical manual of instruction, offering detailed descriptions of the techniques employed by practitioners. My examples ought to be regarded precisely as such—that is, as *examples* of a more general phenomenon that I am placing under philosophical scrutiny. Moreover, the specific disciplines selected for analysis here, while in most cases judged to be especially felicitous choices for the purposes of this study, are also those with which I happen to be most familiar.

Other scholars might expose the historical significance of these examples from any number of interesting critical perspectives, but it was not my intention to do so. I recognize that most of the Japanese samurai, for instance, were crude warriors forced into combat by various economic and political forces and that they had little interest in meditation or spirituality. My book is not about the samurai. It is not a justification for the battles fought by such warriors, and I want emphatically to reject any attempt to romanticize such bloody conflicts. My concerns are of a different sort.

I regard the discourse in most of the texts that I survey here as being essentially prescriptive rather than descriptive. My attention is directed to the logic governing those prescriptive utterances. They supply instruction about how persons ought to live their spiritual lives, not an accurate historical account of how specific persons have actually done so. Maybe very few of the samurai were "loyal" in the way that Royce or Nitobe indicated (chapters 3 and 5 below). Likewise, very few historical Christians could be presented as actual exemplars of the spirituality that Ignatius and Scupoli preached (chapter 4). We do not know if Yagyu Munenori ever attempted to cultivate the spiritual dispositions that Takuan recommended in his letters. My interest is in Takuan's advice, the case he makes for specific values and perspectives, and also in the extent to which that advice might be attractive to certain contemporary practitioners.

All of these texts have a complex effective history. The same text can be used in many different ways and for a great variety of purposes (some of which might be judged harshly and others subsequently praised, depending on who is making the judgment and at what point in time). I found these texts useful to think philosophically with, but I fully recognize that they could be and have been used otherwise.

This inquiry concerning various martial and meditative practices is not intended to suggest that they can all be conflated and treated as a single discipline or that the numerous differences among them are only superficial and so can safely be ignored. The differences are important, whether they point to contrasts in philosophy or in technique. The use of a category like "martial spirituality" does not presuppose some argument about the essential "sameness" of these religious exercises. It is warranted instead by the observation that significant lines of continuity can be traced among the various practices under consideration, links between specific features that are comparable even if they are by no means identical to one another. A different sort of study would be designed to highlight the contrasts. The present inquiry is organized around the task of tracing some of the continuities.[5]

I refer in this book almost exclusively to works in English, in many cases to English translations of texts that were originally produced in other languages. I do so both because of my own scholarly limitations and because these translated texts represent the medium through which most of my readers will have encountered and learned about the martial arts or about various meditative traditions. I have tried to employ gender-neutral language in this discussion. I am sensitive to the fact that the discourse of the martial arts has typically been generated by men and addressed to men, but I would argue that the philosophical and religious significance of this discourse cannot be exhaustively described in terms of gender-related issues. Women as well as men engage in the type of spiritual combat portrayed here.

The book is organized into five chapters. The first supplies a conceptual portrait of aikidō, tracing some of its roots in Japanese traditional and new religions. Enough is known about the origins and development of aikidō that it would be possible to fill in this sketch with considerable (and frequently esoteric) detail.[6] Instead, the desideratum here is a portrait painted with a few broad strokes, emphasizing those features of the subject that link it to the basic themes and questions explored in the book. Attention is focused on the appropriation and transformation of martial images and ideals within aikidō for the purposes of contemporary spiritual practice.

In the second chapter, I present a similar treatment of the Chinese arts of *taijiquan* (*tai chi chuan*) and *baguazhang* (*pa kua chang*), conceived both as martial and as meditative (Daoist) disciplines.[7] That treatment includes an explicit comparison of aikidō with these Chinese arts, both in terms of the techniques and exercises employed in their practice and the religious philosophies that have shaped their development.

The third chapter is divided into three sections. The first supplies a brief consideration of Hindu yoga in relation to the martial ideology embodied in the text of the Bhagavad Gita. The second section treats selected features of the relationship between Zen Buddhism and the martial arts, including the Zen influences on *bushidō* (the Japanese "warrior's code," or ethic). The chapter concludes with a discussion of Islamic jihad as a complex notion embracing both the idea of "holy war" waged against other persons and a more basic concept of moral exertion, of internal spiritual struggle (the "greater jihad").

In chapter 4, I investigate the Christian theology of "spiritual combat," from its earliest traces in the biblical literature through its medieval development, culminating in the martial perspectives on Christian asceticism articulated by Lorenzo Scupoli and Ignatius of Loyola. Again, my primary concerns and questions are philosophical, rather than strictly historical. What is the peculiar logic of this type of theological discourse? What sort of conceptualization of the human spiritual condition must be presupposed if such talk about "combat" is to be meaningful and effective?

These sorts of questions are pursued even more directly in chapter 5, which takes the form of an extended philosophical commentary on the relationship between meditation and martial discipline, drawing especially on sources in classical American pragmatism. These include William James's conception of a "moral equivalent of war," especially as it is articulated in his lectures on "saintliness," published in the *Varieties of Religious Experience*. My commentary is also indebted to Josiah Royce's philosophy of loyalty and to Charles Peirce's scattered but brilliant ruminations on the nature and importance of self-control.

The book concludes with a brief postlude on the concept of *peace* as understood from various religious perspectives and posited as one of the primary goals of dedicated spiritual practice. This peace is something more than the simple absence of conflict. It designates a certain quality of relationship, a positive state of harmony, the realization of which (despite its appearance as a good to be striven for) is always to some extent gratuitous. The fact that some of the arts of war have also been portrayed as "arts of peace" is curious enough to deserve attention. Here peace is not just one of the many predictable, long-range consequences of successful martial activity, nor is it the rhetorical ornament for a simplistic "might makes right" philosophy. Martial arts transformed by the ideal of peace embody a novel understanding of the "enemy," one that requires the development of entirely new strategies of combat and of resistance.

Religious traditions as different as Daoism and Christianity frequently incorporate a paradoxical notion of "power"—of what it means to be powerful or to wield power. This book supplies some consideration of these notions as they shape and inform specific styles of martial spirituality. The type of battle in which such power is displayed is often one waged on an interior landscape, so that the relationship linking inner conflicts to interpersonal ones is also a central topic of concern. This relationship can be articulated in a number of ways, but they all appear to be variations on a common theme: *the essence of control is self-control.* One can prevail against an external foe only if one has first achieved internal self-mastery. From another perspective, external conflicts between persons arise only because conflicts within persons already exist and remain unresolved.

It is not the case, however, that war is something to be explained purely in psychological terms or that all conflicts can be reduced to psychological ones. As William James insisted, there is real evil in the world, whether it manifests itself internally or externally, and there is a moral duty to resist it. For this reason, the martial images and ideals that are employed by those who engage in certain spiritual disciplines cannot be regarded as merely metaphorical: they are accurately descriptive and appropriate to the envisioned purpose of such exercises. That purpose cannot be limited to the use of any meditative or martial art exclusively as a form of self-cultivation, of self-development. There is a self-transcending and a decisively moral dimension to these practices.

If it made no sense to say that there is real evil to be resisted and overcome, then it might be argued that these spiritual practices can and ought to be described in nonmartial terms. Even if certain martial virtues were deemed to be of value for a variety of reasons, there must be ways of inculcating them in persons without pretending to be at war or acting as if one were engaged in combat. War can have devastating consequences: it ought not to be romanticized. James's talk about enjoying the benefits of a moral equivalent of war without having to endure the negative effects of actual human combat will fail to convince those who

regard all instances and "equivalents" of war as necessarily producing bad effects. Any pragmatic defense of these martial disciplines will have to take seriously certain religious claims about
the nature of evil, its various manifestations, and the moral responsibilities that its existence entails.

At the same time, this book is not a defense of any particular
war or of the arguments for a "just war" as it is commonly understood. Conflict among persons is always problematic for
precisely the reasons that this analysis of the spiritual life is
intended to expose. Within the context supplied by certain religious perspectives, the exercise of power is typically manifested
as a certain kind of powerlessness: the self conquers precisely
when it itself is overcome, and the arts of war must always already be conceived as arts of peace.

ONE

The Way of Spiritual Harmony

Aikidō is a martial art created by Morihei Ueshiba (1883–1969) in the twentieth century, but with deep roots in classical styles of jūjutsu and Japanese swordsmanship. Its practitioners emphasize the strategy of blending with an attacker's aggressive energy rather than responding to brute force with force. The result is a martial art that is distinguished by its beautiful, flowing movements, embodying an attitude of peaceful relaxation, without abandoning its purpose as a form of self-defense.

Trained at a very early age in budō, the various arts of war, Ueshiba was a soldier in the Japanese army during the conflict with Russia that broke out in February 1904. Both during and after his military tour of duty, he studied martial arts in a number of prominent dōjōs, acquiring a master's proficiency with the sword and the spear as well as in various styles of unarmed combat. In later years he was deeply influenced by the trauma of events during and surrounding World War II. Drawing upon all of his training and experience, Ueshiba created and gradually developed aikidō, a martial art grounded in traditional budō but influenced by the Shintō and Buddhist meditative disciplines of Ueshiba's native Japan and blended with principles drawn from his long association with the Japanese new religion Ōmoto-kyō. Conceiving it as a means of producing harmony, both within the self and among persons in conflict, he described aikidō as an "art of peace" and he declared the true samurai to be "one who serves and adheres to the power of love." In 1942, Ueshiba wrote that "The Way of the warrior has been misunderstood as a means to kill and destroy others. Those who seek competition are making a grave mistake. To smash, injure, or destroy is the worst sin a human being can commit. The real way of a warrior is to prevent slaughter—it is the art of peace, the power of love."[1]

Despite the apparent oddness of this characterization of the art of the warrior as a practice of love, Ueshiba insisted that his perspective faithfully represented the essence of traditional budō. That essence, he contended, is typically obscured and corrupted by the ignorant, often self-serving behavior of many contemporary teachers and practitioners. Ueshiba intended his aikidō to be a recovery and a rejuvenation of the authentic spirit of the martial arts. "In true budō, there are no enemies. True budō is a function of love. It is not for killing or fighting but to foster all things and bring them to fruition. Love protects and nourishes life. Without love nothing can be accomplished. Aikidō is the manifestation of love."[2]

It is a natural impulse to question the motivation for this type of discourse, to challenge the sincerity or authenticity of this portrayal of a fighting art as an essentially peaceful practice. It is reasonable to conjecture, for example, that Ueshiba's talk about peace is rhetoric designed to meet the needs of a booming export market for the Japanese martial arts after the war. While there may be an element of truth here, Ueshiba's pacifism was clearly a pre-war phenomenon and appears to have been firmly grounded in his religious convictions, so that the picture is more complicated than such a conjecture allows. Furthermore, not content simply to articulate the philosophy of aikidō as a set of abstract principles, Ueshiba struggled to embody those principles in the actual practice of the art. Toward this end, in the period after World War II he significantly edited the vast syllabus of martial techniques inherited from the various forms of classical Japanese jūjutsu in which he was accomplished. This editing process resulted in a dramatic simplification of the art, involving elimination of those techniques considered to be excessively violent and destructive, even lethal. In this modified practice, an emphasis was placed on relatively "soft" techniques—the art of blending with an attacker's vital energy (ki), redirecting that energy in order to harmonize with it and so render it harmless. The strategy was to "enter deeply into an attack and neutralize it as you draw that misdirected attack into your own sphere."[3]

This strategy will require more careful analysis. So, too, will Ueshiba's potentially misleading assertion that there are "no enemies" in genuine budō. Clearly, he was not ignoring or denying the possibility that a person might be seriously threatened by someone wishing to do harm. Moreover, he recognized the importance of confrontation with some "enemy" for the purpose of awakening the human spirit from its slumber, strengthening and focusing it. "At the instant a warrior faces an enemy," he observed, "all things serve to make the teachings more focused."[4] Ideally, the encounter with a hostile other serves as a stimulus, totally engaging the self, bringing it to a state of heightened awareness.

Nevertheless, the most dangerous enemy, the only enemy that must be defeated, is "the mind of contention that we harbor within." Ueshiba addressed this challenge consistently in his writings and utterances. "The penetrating brilliance of swords wielded by followers of the Way strikes at the evil enemy lurking deep within their own souls and bodies. The art of peace is not easy. It is a fight to the finish, the slaying of evil desires and all falsehood within. On occasion the voice of peace resounds like thunder, jolting human beings out of their stupor."[5]

The "voice of peace" may be embodied, paradoxically, in hostile or aggressive acts and gestures, but it is itself a summons to respond with love, in a spirit of reconciliation. "Opponents confront us continually, but actually there is no opponent there."[6] Rather than being a naïve denial of the existence of potential enemies, Ueshiba's perspective called for a transformation of one's typical pattern of response to such aggressors. Jesus' challenging admonition to his disciples that they should "love their enemies" is a moral teaching that Ueshiba strenuously endorsed. With regard to Jesus' advice that one should "turn the other cheek" when struck by another person, Ueshiba altered the

strategy for students of aikidō, recommending that they antici-
pate the blow and turn before being struck (a reference to the circular, turning techniques *[tenkan]* so typical of aikidō practice).

If Ueshiba perceived aikidō as the "manifestation of love,"
this love was not to be understood, in sentimental terms, as a
pure emotion or simple feeling response. It is a powerful disposition both shaping and shaped by human volition, one that
can be developed gradually through practice (and this is "not
easy"). Learning to love one's enemies requires more than a
change in the way that one feels about them. It marks a transformation of one's whole way of being in the world, a new way
of being in relation to others. Following the path that Ueshiba
sketched in his teachings would require the cultivation of specific martial virtues: "Loyalty and devotion lead to bravery. Bravery leads to the spirit of self-sacrifice. The spirit of self-sacrifice
creates trust in the power of love."[7] The rigorous training prescribed for practitioners of aikidō is not limited in scope, however, to the task of "polishing the spirit." It is also necessary to
"toughen the body," not as a completely separate exercise but as
a means of facilitating spiritual progress. Physical endurance and
vigor remain important even when the primary goal is no longer
to conquer some dangerous human opponent. In Ueshiba's
view, it was necessary for warriors to understand the body as a
"vehicle to train the mind, calm the spirit, and find goodness
and beauty."[8]

The intended initial effect of diligent aikidō practice is a powerful self-transformation; but this effect can have important ethical, social, and political consequences. The "calm spirit" is one
now poised to bring peace into the world, to restore harmony to
relationships now poisoned by discord.

Ueshiba's postwar transformation of his martial practice was
symbolized by his creation of a new name for that discipline.
Earlier designations—first *aiki-jutsu*, later *aiki-budō*—were replaced by *aikidō*, a word consisting in the Japanese of three char-

acters and meaning literally the way *(dō)* of harmony *(ai)* with spirit or vital energy *(ki)*. Each of these characters is multivalent. For example, ki is manifested in the human body as breath, as the source of life and vitality. On this level, *aiki* can represent a state of being in harmony with oneself, a coordination of mind and body that is one of the goals of most forms of breathing meditation. It might also refer to the successful blending with another person's energy (as in the case of skillful dance partners). But the concept of ki can have a more general metaphysical and cosmological significance. Here it is appropriate to speak about the ki of the universe, a primordial ki that arose from the original void and empowers or animates all things. This was a religiously meaningful concept for Ueshiba and one that has deep roots in various Asian philosophical traditions. In his view, the spirit of the universe was divine; correspondingly, *aiki* came to designate a fundamental condition of being in harmony with the divine reality.

The notion of what constitutes such a harmony is itself variously described in Ueshiba's utterances, as well as in much of the later literature about aikidō. Moreover, these utterances were typically aphoristic, often poetic, and admittedly vague. Nevertheless, in his later philosophical reflections, Ueshiba tended increasingly to analyze ai as a harmony produced by the power of love. The divine reality was itself frequently personalized and described as a deity. Consequently, aikidō can be portrayed as a way or path devoted to the love of God. At the same time, for Ueshiba, "love is God's essence," so that the practice of aikidō involves an imitation, ideally a "manifestation," of the divine reality. "Victory is to harmonize self and other, to link yourself to the Divine, to yoke yourself to Divine Love, to become the universe itself."[9]

Despite the vagueness—indeed, the obscurity—of many of the religious teachings that Ueshiba communicated in his lectures and his poetry, it is important that a summary of them be given to supply the appropriate context for an analysis of aikidō as a spiritual discipline. Yet it is the discipline itself, its distinctive practices and techniques, that represents Ueshiba's true legacy. His religious philosophy is more eloquently articulated in physical form and movement, in embodied strategies of combat and resistance, than in any surviving poem or text. Some of these practices were derived from the religious traditions that informed Ueshiba's spirituality, much as his martial techniques were drawn from classical schools of jūjutsu. In each case, it is the logic of Ueshiba's transformation or adaptation of technique for specific purposes that deserves careful attention here.

Sitting and standing meditation were important elements of Ueshiba's training in the martial arts. It is reported that he would typically engage in this sort of meditation prior to physical training, but also as an independent exercise and sometimes for extended periods of time.[10] Powerfully influenced by his experiences with Ōmoto-kyō, the initial purpose of this practice was conceived as *chinkon-kishin*, the use of the breath to calm the mind and body, to "settle the spirits." This settling into the *hara*, the center of one's being, was understood, at the same time, to be a return to the divine center of the cosmos. In this manner, it was believed, the ki of heaven and the ki of earth mingle and are harmonized.

More than simply a restoration of calmness, breathing meditation was also a ritual of purification for Ueshiba, an act of *misogi*. A traditional practice within the context of Japanese religious life, misogi can have multiple layers of meaning. At one level, it is a rite of physical purification, usually involving water (often immersion in a natural body of water or standing beneath a waterfall). But spiritual impurities are to be purged in the process as well, forcibly expelled from the body with each exhalation. The breath is an indispensable tool for the purposes of misogi, exhalation and inhalation supplying the mechanism for the fresh circulation of vital ki into and throughout the body.

Ueshiba supplemented basic forms of sitting and standing meditation with exercises influenced by his practice of aikidō. A common exercise involved wielding the four-foot staff, or *jō*, one of the two basic weapons employed in aikidō training, the other being the wooden sword, or *bokken*. (Many of the empty-handed techniques in aikidō are patterned on movements typically associated with the use of the staff or sword.) *Misogi-no-jō* was a method of purification utilizing the jō in a dance-like series of movements and postures. It would often conclude with the jō held in both hands and pointed skyward, literally drawing down the ki of heaven while uniting the spirit of heaven and of earth within the solidly rooted body of the aikidōka. This creative employment of the staff in misogi-no-jō represents an important link between the traditional Shintō or Buddhist exercises that shaped Ueshiba's religious perspective and his maturest conception of aikidō as a spiritual discipline. Here a standard training weapon is transformed into an element of sacred ritual.

The Shintō practices of *furitama* and *torifune* (or *funakogi*) were incorporated by Ueshiba into his aikidō training. Furitama is a type of standing meditation with hands held in front of the body at the level of the hara. The hands are clasped softly, as if holding something tiny and fragile, and at the same time are gently but vigorously shaken. With the left hand over the right hand, its primary purpose is *chinkon*, a settling of spirits and collecting of the fragmented elements of the self; with right hand over left, it is intended as misogi. Torifune, commonly known as the "rowing exercise," remains a standard practice in aikidō dōjōs throughout the world. Kisshomaru Ueshiba, the founder's son, described it in simple terms as an exercise in which "one stands with one leg forward and one leg back, clenching both hands as if they held oars. The hips become the center of a repetitious forward-and-backward movement that resembles rowing. Throughout the back-and-forth movements, ki is maintained in the centrum as a method of unifying mind and body."[11]

Torifune can be understood exclusively in terms of its practical physical significance for a student training in martial techniques. As such, it is designed to develop the practitioner's ability to organize movements around the body's center of gravity, to remain centered and stable even when weight is being shifted rapidly from one foot to another (as might be the case if a person were to be shoved, struck, or pulled). For Ueshiba, however, this practice clearly had a greater significance. It was a "centering" exercise, to be sure, but in a fully spiritual as well as a biomechanical sense. Conceived in this fashion, it is a very basic and invaluable form of moving meditation, intended to achieve effects similar to those associated with certain forms of sitting or standing meditation, but here under conditions that may enhance its value. It is an important accomplishment if one can achieve a peaceful state of mind and enhance the flow of ki through the body as one sits calmly in a state of repose (for example, as in the traditional Zen Buddhist practice of zazen). But if that condition is sacrificed as soon as the practitioner begins to move about or interact with other people (including those who are aggressive or hostile), then it may be judged to be of limited value. Aikidō training is designed to prolong and stabilize such a peaceful condition; torifune prepares the student for interpersonal encounters that will occur both on the mats during training and in daily experiences outside of the dōjō.

All of these forms of meditation—sitting, standing, or moving, those intended for purposes of calming, centering, or purification—are practices of controlled breathing or paying attention to breathing. In a great variety of philosophical and religious traditions, breathing is perceived as a fundamental mode of interaction between the inner and the outer, the personal and the cosmic. It occurs naturally, as something that happens to one in a way that is partially determined by involuntary biological processes and partially by objective conditions (e.g., an absence of oxygen on a mountain peak or in a stuffy room; an abundance of fresh air on a crisp autumn morning). Yet breathing is also a process that one can become conscious of and to some extent control. Breath, though an invisible phenomenon, is the essential source of biological life and well-being, and thus it is both a spiritual and a physical reality. For Ueshiba, it was the perfect embodiment of ki.

Indeed, the concepts of breath *(kokyū)* and spirit *(ki)* are very closely related, not only in Shintō and Buddhism but also in Daoist and Hindu philosophy; one can even make a strong case for Christianity.[12] Ueshiba certainly affirmed this connection, while maintaining a subtle distinction between them. "*Ki,*" he said, "is the nuclear force, the supreme creative power at the center of all things"; whereas breathing, "the yin and yang of respiration, . . . diversifies and cleanses all things with the exchange, the separation and reunion, of this power. Creation within the body, within the spirit, and within the universe is the living breath of God's love. Respiration is the driving force of life. This is the power of *kokyū.*"[13]

The present discussion of aikidō is intended to show that as the art evolved from its earliest to its most developed form, Ueshiba increasingly regarded martial exercises as constituting a spiritual practice—that is, martial art as meditation. Misogino-jō and torifune are useful examples in this regard: the former employs a weapon as an extension of the self in meditation, the latter transforms a Shintō ritual into a martial arts exercise. In every relevant case, the continuous emphasis on breath and breathing supplies an important point of contact between sitting, standing, and martial meditation.

The examples already explored are exercises typically performed by individuals. *Kokyū-dōsa,* on the other hand, is a very basic and, potentially, deeply meditative aikidō exercise that involves interaction with another person. While sitting in the posture traditionally used in martial arts *(seiza),* one partner gently but firmly holds the wrists of the other. The person thus held responds by consciously breathing but also by moving, organizing movements around the hara, from where the breath originates, while gently moving and controlling the "attacker." This is not at all a wrestling match, a test of brute strength, but rather an exercise designed to allow a practitioner, with the partner's assistance, to become more deeply aware of the power that is embedded in the center of the body. At the same time, there is a blending with the partner's breath and energy, a deep awareness of it in the interaction. Kokyū-dōsa is intended to have a calming effect on the participants, and in many dōjōs it is the exercise with which a training session concludes.

Most techniques in aikidō that do not involve the bending or manipulation of joints are known as *kokyū-nage* (sometimes *kokyū-hō*), breath or timing throws. These consist of all those techniques that are designed exclusively around the strategy of feeling, blending with, and then redirecting, an attacker's ki as it is embodied in a strike, push, or pull. Yet in an important sense, for Ueshiba, kokyū was the essence of aikidō, and all aikidō techniques could be conceived as kokyū-nage. Constant awareness of the relationship between one's own hara and that of an attacker allows the aikidōka to control a potentially dangerous situation with a minimal amount of pain inflicted on shoulder, elbow, or wrist, even in techniques that require the manipulation of these joints.

This awareness consists in a state of mindfulness, an attentiveness that can be maintained at levels ranging from the fairly superficial to the extraordinary. Ueshiba was famous for his ability to achieve a profoundly concentrated state, to realize on the mats and when under attack a form of awareness typical of what spiritual adepts might achieve in prolonged sitting meditation. The reports of Ueshiba's ability to sidestep bullets fired from a gun by sensing their speed and direction may be more relevant to a hagiographic tale than to a scholarly account of the man and his art, but film of Ueshiba performing aikidō in his later years (he died at the age of eighty-six) supplies clear evidence of the extent to which kokyū-nage had become the distilled essence of his martial art. Approached by multiple attackers *(randori)*, Ueshiba seemed to sense each movement, responding in subtle but effective ways in order to maintain both perfect self-control and control of the attackers, sometimes barely touching them— or not touching them at all.

Like the concept of ki, kokyū can take on a broad cosmological or metaphysical significance in Ueshiba's teachings. Against the backdrop provided by Ōmoto-kyō mysticism, one can portray the divine reality as literally breathing all things into existence or, since breath is manifested audibly in speech, as speaking things into existence and giving them life. A person imitates this cosmic phenomenon in the recitation of the *kotodama*, sacred words (actually syllables) in Shintō belief that hold the key to the secrets of divine creation.[14] Ueshiba was extensively trained in and deeply committed to this practice, pursuing it in esoteric detail and adapting it to his own philosophy and purposes. He devoted considerable time and energy to repeating the syllables of the kotodama like a mantra; indeed, this exercise is in some ways comparable to the Hindu practice of *japam* or Roman Catholic prayer in the form of recitation of a rosary.[15] In aikidō it can also be related to the sharply released breath in the occasional shout of the martial artist *(kiai)*, intended to enhance power and effectiveness in executing technique. Of course, from the perspective that Ueshiba sketched, this represented a creative and life-affirming act rather than a destructive one, even if the technique was potentially devastating.

How is the religious meaning of these diverse exercises, all organized around the awareness and control of breathing, to be understood? Ueshiba instructed his students: "Rise early in the morning to greet the sun. Breathe in and let yourself soar to the ends of the universe; breathe out and bring the cosmos back inside. Next breathe up all the fecundity and vibrancy of the earth. Finally, blend the Breath of Earth with that of your own, becoming the Breath of Life itself. Your body and mind will be gladdened, depression and heartache will dissipate, and you will be filled with gratitude."[16]

The mystical tone of this instruction, characteristic of so

many of Ueshiba's utterances, is of less interest here than the specific conclusion that he draws. The goal of the practice is to develop an appropriate sense of *gratitude*. Chinkon-kishin calms the mind, centers it and focuses it; misogi purifies the mind of distractions and impurities; but ideally, the result of both forms of meditation is a deepening of awareness that fosters powerful feelings of gratitude *(kansha)*.[17] These feelings have a certain religious quality since the gratitude being fostered here is gratitude for nothing in particular, and so for everything—for all beings as well for the fact of being itself. At a certain level of vagueness, it is possible to argue that a fundamental religious attitude, characteristic of a great variety of traditions with diverse histories and theologies, essentially consists of gratitude. This attitude is rooted in a vital awareness that existence itself is gratuitous; to see the world clearly is to perceive everything as a gift.

Aikidō training, conceived as spiritual practice, is intended to develop such an awareness in practitioners. One of the fundamental techniques in aikidō, in some respects as basic as kokyū-nage, is *shihō-nage*, the "four directions throw." It is a projection technique deriving its distinctive footwork and body movements from Japanese swordsmanship, and it can be effectively utilized in response to a great variety of attacks. Its spiritual significance consists in its being a symbolic expression of gratitude—indeed, of four basic kinds of gratitude: gratitude directed toward the spirit of the cosmos, toward one's ancestors, toward the whole of nature, and toward other human beings.[18] Successful performance of this technique requires that one do it mindfully, with a deep sense of kansha and not in a fashion that will merely achieve its intended martial effect. Thus, shihō-nage, like the exercises already described and discussed, is an important form of moving meditation. (It was reported by a number of Ueshiba's students to be the master's favorite technique.)

The fostering of gratitude, however, is by no means a project that can be confined to one technique or to periods of sitting meditation and ritual purification. The desideratum is that this attitude should pervade all of practice in the dōjō until, gradually, it becomes a powerful disposition, habitually shaping one's everyday interactions with persons and things in the world. Aikidō is distinguished from many other martial arts by the fact that its training is organized around practice with a partner. There are solo exercises in aikidō and some weapons *kata* (forms), but these do not constitute the bulk of training for aikidōka as they do for practitioners of other martial systems. Aikidō is an essentially interpersonal activity involving *uke* (the person who initiates an attack) and *nage* (the one who performs an appropriate technique in response). The crucial point that needs to be emphasized here is that both partners *receive* something in the encounter. Nage is the recipient of an attack, which under most circumstances could be interpreted as a hostile, even hateful gesture. The philosophy of aikidō supplies an alternative interpretive matrix for this event, allowing the person attacked to perceive it as a gift, literally as a gift of ki, of uke's own vital energy. That gift is to be received with open hands (clenched fists are rare in aikidō practice), as well as with an open heart and a relaxed spirit, in gratitude. Of course, this kind of perspective is a plausible one, in part because the experienced aikidōka will be trained to deal with that energy—will know how to blend with it, use it, and so avoid or prevent its potentially destructive consequences.

Uke receives something as well: specifically, the aikidō technique that is performed by nage, which typically results in the attacker being thrown and taking a fall *(ukemi)*. It is easy for a beginning student to focus attention on nage's role in training and to identify it with the practice of aikidō. It would seem, after all, that this is the person who is actually doing the aikidō; uke is present in the encounter only to simulate an attack for nage's purposes, while patiently waiting a turn. Ueshiba, however, denied that there is any asymmetry in the significance of the roles played by each partner. Moreover, the skills needed to perform successfully the role of uke are typically the ones that are first taught to a novice student. This is the case not only because such skills must be inculcated before aikidō technique can be performed without a great risk of injury. It is also true that there is something of paramount spiritual significance involved in the art of "taking a fall," of receiving technique in a graceful and relaxed manner, with a certain humility, and, again, in a spirit of gratitude.

One might argue that only in the artificial environment created by the dōjō is it possible to perceive an attack or a counterattack as a gift and to respond, to either, with gratitude; after all, in the dōjō both persons are in fact partners, engaged in a friendly pursuit, helping one another to learn the basic principles of a martial art. Yet it seems clear that the philosophy of aikidō articulated by Ueshiba and many of his followers is intended to place more radical demands on its practitioners. Violent attacks encountered anywhere and initiated by anyone are to be interpreted as potential gifts and to be greeted with a gentle, even loving response. This will seem like an unrealistic and dangerous prescription for the aikidōka unless two presuppositions are maintained. It must first be presupposed that one possesses the martial skill necessary to transform angry and dangerous encounters into ones that are peaceful and benign. (Ueshiba sought to modify and develop techniques precisely for this purpose.) Secondly, in order for such a prescription to be meaningful, it must be assumed that training in martial arts is always already a form of spiritual discipline, a training of the spirit as well as of the body or, better, a training of the spirit through the body (more on this below).

Blending with an attack is usually accomplished first by moving, sometimes in a very subtle fashion, off the line of attack. There is no brute clash of forces in aikidō, no direct confrontation. One of the two basic strategies for moving off-line characterizes all of those techniques that are performed tenkan. This involves stepping forward and slightly outside of an attack while pivoting and turning 180 degrees. After executing such a strategy, nage will be shoulder-to-shoulder with uke as a kind of mirror image, now facing in the same direction. As a self-defense tactic it is efficacious, quickly moving nage off the line of attack and setting up any number of possible responses. Yet the tenkan movement is also symbolically expressive, eloquently describing a new and potentially harmonious relationship between uke and nage. At the moment of attack, they stood opposed to one another, each perceiving a world with a distinctive horizon, but in a sense blinded (at least in that moment) to what the other was able to see. Tenkan represents a form of conversion, a literal and symbolic turning away from confrontation with the other in order to experience what the other sees. Now uke and nage share a world.

There is no magic involved in such a conversion, no automatic and immediate transformation of enemies into comrades. Yet the transformation is nonetheless a real one and contains within itself at least the seeds of a possible reconciliation. The strategy enacted here represents a refusal on the part of one person to interpret a situation in the terms apparently supplied by another, to see the encounter as a necessarily violent and hostile one. Once again, if this refusal is to represent something other than a naïve and dangerous type of self-delusion, then it must be rooted in a deep awareness of those conditions that shape the present situation as it unfolds. One who responds in this way must possess the ability not only to perceive but also creatively to transform those conditions. The primary purpose of training in aikidō (as Ueshiba articulated it) is the cultivation of just such an ability.

Here the concept of enemy becomes problematic; if not rendered meaningless altogether, its meaning is certainly complicated. As already noted, Ueshiba's talk about enemies is seemingly paradoxical. He speaks of confronting the enemy, of the spiritual significance of that encounter, yet he insists that there are in fact "no enemies"; even when surrounded by aggressors, there is "no opponent there." One way of understanding these teachings involves the consideration of persons and relationships within an appropriate temporal context. *Enemy* does not designate the fixed essence of some person or group; rather, it describes a certain quality of the relationship between persons, one that can change with time and vary with circumstances. To speak about "born enemies" may make some limited sense if the reference is to certain animal species that, given their inherited physical characteristics and instinctive patterns of behavior, are likely to compete for resources within a particular ecosystem. But human beings always have a history. When individuals are born into human communities that are mutually hostile to one another, these communities have a distinctive history, one that has shaped the present conflict. Moreover, membership in a particular community need not be the only factor determining the quality of a given person's attitudes and relationships.

An attack (whether physical, verbal, or some other kind) can manifest varying degrees of hostility. Some encounters are ambiguous; there may even be so much ambiguity that one may not be entirely sure that it is in fact an "attack." In such a case, to respond with hostility may actually precipitate a conflict where there was in fact none, or it may fan a few sparks of anger into a violent conflagration. Even in cases that are entirely unambiguous, a gentle, loving response can sometimes succeed in defusing an encounter and transforming a relationship. That was Ueshiba's teaching. It does not presuppose blindness to the other's anger and intended violence. It does involve the recognition that emotions and intentions are labile, not permanently fixed, but subject to change and vulnerable to influence.

When Ueshiba talked about enemies, he preferred to talk about the "enemy within." There is a certain sense in which the encounter with any enemy is always also an encounter with an internal foe, sometimes manifesting itself as anger or hatred, sometimes as fear, even in the form of distractions, but always fueled by the ego's selfish desires. The primary goal of training in budō is the conquering of this enemy, the achievement through continuous discipline of a high degree of self-control. The experience of anger or fear is typically concomitant with the experience of another person's aggressive actions or demeanor. Control of the self is the key to achieving control of the interpersonal situation. This observation, while it can be quite simply stated, actually requires some extended consideration.

In the first place, self-control can be achieved on a variety of levels, so that it represents both a physical and spiritual objective. The less control one has over one's body and physical movements, the greater the risk of injuring oneself or another. Martial arts techniques are most effective when they are executed with precision, with the body perfectly balanced and movements organized efficiently around the center of gravity. As in dance or athletic competition, successful performance in the martial arts requires an appropriately high level of physical self-control.

However, physical skill and training are not irrelevant to the task of understanding aikidō as a spiritual discipline. In fact, this kind of physical self-control can certainly be symbolic or expressive of a harmonious spiritual or psychic condition. More importantly, it can help to facilitate the latter so that the effecting of an appropriate posture, flowing movements, and regular, relaxed breathing are clearly all strategies for calming the mind or "settling the spirits." One does not have to be trained either in meditation or in the martial arts in order to recognize that the use of controlled breathing, in particular, is an especially effective way to combat feelings of fear or anger as they arise or to enhance concentration. Initially, then, a relaxed and peaceful physical demeanor may be symbolic of a psychological or spiritual condition that does not yet in fact obtain. Adopting the appropriate physical disposition helps to precipitate correspondingly appropriate feelings and attitudes, so that self-control consists in performing actions that are primarily effective for and symbolic of some *future version* of the self.[19]

As already indicated, this analysis is not intended to suggest that there are really no enemies to be resisted, no evil that represents a genuine threat or danger to the self. On the contrary, this danger is so significant that it must be combated on multiple fronts, the battleground encompassing both an interior and an exterior landscape. Within the spiritual universe depicted by Ueshiba, hatred, fear, anger, and distraction are accurately to be regarded as weapons wielded by the enemy, strategies employed against the self that are even more threatening to the self than a sword wielded by a flesh-and-blood opponent. That sword can kill the body, but anger, hatred, and so forth hold the potential to cause spiritual death; they can cut more deeply than any physical object, poisoning not only the self at its core but also everything and everyone that the self touches. Furthermore, in order to control the attacker's sword (as opposed to simply destroying the attacker), a degree of physical and spiritual self-mastery must already have been achieved.

There are, then, "no enemies" in genuine budō in the quite specific sense that the enemy is never to be identified with a person or group. The real evil to be resisted manifests itself as a disharmony between persons or within the self—quite literally, as a lack of love. Talk about an enemy best describes a certain quality of relationship, rather than the fixed quality of some person or thing. Such a way of talking does not eliminate the threat of evil, but it does suggest alternative strategies for resisting it, while helping to explain how Ueshiba could conceive of budō as the "manifestation of love." At a minimum, such strategies involved controlling and rendering harmless any sort of violent attacker, drawing "the misdirected attack into your own sphere." More positively, the goal in aikidō is to touch the attacker's heart and mind, to transform entrenched feelings and attitudes, often by signifying in physical movement and disposition the possibility of an entirely different interpretation of the encounter.

The tension produced by combining talk about "enemies" and "combat" with discourse about "love" and "harmony" is characteristic of the type of martial spirituality that forms the present object of inquiry. That tension was creative in Ueshiba's case because thoughts about the enemy, on his account, help to generate a certain heightened awareness, the sort of attentiveness, in fact, that love requires. To refuse or suppress such thoughts altogether is to risk falling into a stupor—the kind of slumber that can become spiritual death. The spiritual task requires a warrior's vigilance because it involves the element of risk that every warrior confronts.

Such a risk is never purely psychological or merely subjective. This is true in the same sense that it is true to assert that self-control is never simply about control of the self. Success or failure for the person engaging in spiritual discipline is to be measured not solely or even primarily in terms of the degree of individual psychic harmony that such discipline produces. Aikidō was an "art of peace" for Ueshiba precisely because he saw its practice as a powerful means for sustaining or creating harmony among persons, as well as between persons and their natural environment. Indeed, this practice was itself essentially interpersonal and interactive, organized around the dynamic relationship between uke and nage and requiring a constant awareness of surroundings and circumstances.

Moreover, interactions can begin and relationships can have significant histories long before there is any physical contact between persons, even developing between persons who never establish such contact at all. This explains the subtle but nevertheless great importance attached in aikidō philosophy to the principle of *ma-ai*, or "proper distancing." It is a principle that ought not to be reduced in its application to an understanding of the optimal distance between nage and uke for the purpose of executing a specific martial technique. Rather, it involves a deeper understanding of the circumstances that affect any particular encounter, an awareness of how position and distance shape that encounter long before it becomes one of conflict. Indeed, if the principle of ma-ai is applied with great expertise,

perhaps such conflict can be avoided, or at least its most dangerous effects can be perceived in advance and thus softened or
neutralized.

In summary: since Ueshiba perceived the body as a "vehicle
to train the mind," physical exercises in aikidō can be understood as a means of "polishing" the spirit. This represents a fundamental point of contact between meditation and the martial
arts.[20] Since the body and mind form a unity, one is able to effect
a transformation of the latter by working with and on the former.
Physical habits and bodily self-control are related both causally
and symbolically to certain inner dispositions, to specific habits
of thought and feeling. Aikidō exercises, whether performed in
solitude or with a partner, are not merely preparatory for some
spiritual practice but can themselves be conceived as meditation. Moreover, this kind of training, even when it is solitary, is
always to be understood as a social practice, a rigorous form of
moral training. It is a way of training oneself how to be in the
world, in relation to other persons and things in the world. It is
a *martial* exercise because evil, a violent, disruptive force, manifests itself as a constant threat to such relations. Just as the body
cannot be isolated from the mind, the self cannot be abstracted
from the web of relations within which it is enmeshed. The
battle against this evil, for Ueshiba, was not simply an act of self-
preservation; it was preeminently an exercise in moral responsibility, the caring for and protection of others, and hence an act of
love.

Ueshiba's poetic aphorisms often contain teachings about
love in both its human and divine manifestations. And like
much human discourse about love—discourse representative of
a variety of cultures and traditions—Ueshiba's teachings display
a certain characteristic vagueness. That vagueness is partially
mitigated, however, by two factors that distinguish Ueshiba's instruction concerning aikidō, both of which have already been
noted. In the first place, much of Ueshiba's talk about love is
striking, even startling, because of the martial context in which

it is embedded. His are the poems of a soldier; love is the sword with which the warrior strikes at the heart of the enemy, and so genuine budō is always the practice of love. Secondly, that talk is consistently translated into, embodied, and so actually *interpreted* in physical movements and exercises. Any commentary on the philosophy of aikidō must include the analysis of such exercises as well as of Ueshiba's utterances. This observation supplies the guiding rationale for much of the preceding discussion, and several important conclusions of a general nature can be drawn as a consequence.

The philosophy of aikidō, in the first place, is distinguished by its pragmatism.[21] Both as a physical and a spiritual discipline, the goal of aikidō is habit formation; that is, the development in the practitioner of certain distinctive habits of posture, movement, and interaction, as well as corresponding habits of thought, feeling, and volition. It is easy to caricature Ueshiba's talk about love as romantic and naïve, as the quasi-mystical invocation of an abstract harmony bestowed on persons "from above," almost magically transforming violent encounters into happy, peaceful ones. On the contrary, the work of love for Ueshiba was a sweaty business, requiring a tremendous amount of hard work, discipline, and self-sacrifice. The art of peace is "not easy"; rather, it is an arduous task, involving the development through constant practice of powerful physical and spiritual dispositions that must then constantly be tested in human encounters, both those contrived within the dōjō and those that occur on the path of everyday life. Ueshiba's pragmatism is further evidenced by his willingness to edit techniques and alter his practice on the basis of his experience. As a martial art, aikidō evolved tremendously during the lifetime of the founder, and it has continued to undergo numerous transformations since his death in 1969.

In addition, and partially as a consequence of this pragmatism, the art of aikidō must also be conceived as an exercise in semiotic; that is, as an art of sign interpretation, one that presupposes the development of specific habits of interpretation. Every martial artist must be skilled at reading the intentions of others based on cues supplied by physical expression, demeanor, posture, and gesture. In the case of aikidō, this interpretive task is complicated by the additional goal of generating multiple interpretive possibilities for any given situation, supplying alternative frames of reference that encompass the future as well as the past and present. One must become skilled at interpreting and then reinterpreting an encounter, creatively envisioning peaceful outcomes. Such interpretation is not the activity of a merely passive observer but involves the aikidōka as both the subject and the object of interpretation. Self-understanding is often a key prerequisite for understanding the conditions that create potential conflicts, just as self-control is frequently the key to resolving them. Moreover, the aikidōka may be required to "interpret" a particular situation with hands and feet and hara, in the form of bodily movements, rather than with thoughts expressed in words.

The development of physical flexibility is important in order for the martial artist to be able to execute techniques properly or to respond to an attack in a relaxed and efficient manner. So, too, a certain spiritual flexibility seems essential to the successful practice of aikidō as an art of interpretation. Here, again, the physical condition signifies the spiritual, and the cultivation of the former (in the practice of yoga as well as in aikidō) is intended ideally to have certain psychological and spiritual benefits. Flexibility is, in fact, a physical metaphor for the quality of mind that philosophers have more typically tended to describe as an attitude of detachment.[22] The inflexible person is one who is rigidly or doggedly attached to certain ways of thinking or acting. To develop spiritual flexibility is to detach oneself, to relax the grip of these dominant modes of behavior, much as physical flexibility requires the stretching and relaxation of dangerously tight or rigid muscles, tendons, and ligaments.

For Ueshiba, the "enemy within" is victorious to the extent

that this relaxed but concentrated state of mind cannot be achieved, that is, to the extent that the rigid, inflexible self endures, blinded by egoistic impulses, refusing to be sacrificed. This is the heart of violence, the source of all disharmony, of both internal and interpersonal conflicts. Ueshiba understood true victory as "self-victory" and the victorious self as one that is detached, flexible, free from bondage to desire, and so both peaceful and "empty": "Return to the source and leave behind all self-centered thoughts, petty desires, and anger. Those who are possessed by nothing possess everything. If you have not linked yourself to true emptiness, you will never understand the Art of Peace."[23]

The peace that is the goal of aikidō is not merely a state that is "empty" of all conflict, superficially conceived. It is a positive and dynamic state, one that involves constant change and interaction, a work of love that results in the harmony of interests and intentions. Practitioners of the art are disposed to embrace all things as a gift, to reject or destroy nothing. The linking to "true emptiness" that makes this a possibility involves the development of a certain habit of detachment that governs all other habits and tendencies, even those inculcated in the process of rigorous aikidō training, softening their hold, undermining their hegemony. No one technique, no single response, can ever be determined in advance for a particular situation. Rather, "the best strategy relies upon an unlimited set of responses."[24] This indeterminacy is not to be understood as chaos or a sheer lack of purpose. For one who is appropriately disposed—detached, attentive, and self-controlled—it is the exercise of an authentic freedom.

The Ōmoto-kyō religion, with which Morihei Ueshiba was associated for much of his adult life, was characterized in the early phases of its development by certain apocalyptic tendencies. Its leaders prophesied the coming of a new age of world peace and prosperity and its adherents lived both hopefully waiting for that golden age and vigorously working toward its realization. Ueshiba's philosophy was shaped by a number of influences, both classical and contemporary, but it clearly bears the stamp of Ōmoto-kyō doctrine and practice.

As a result, aikidō became for him a method of self-cultivation, with an emphasis on self-effort and personal responsibility, on the positive role that every individual can play in bringing about a harmonious world order.[25] At the same time, the peace envisioned was a spiritual reality, the work of a divine power that transcends the individual person. It was to be anticipated, rather than achieved, or, more accurately, to be achieved only insofar as one served disinterestedly as the instrument of the divine. The emphasis on self-cultivation was balanced in Ueshiba's perspective by a warrior's talk about the necessity for heroic self-sacrifice, for loyalty to something greater than the self. Strenuous training of body and continuous polishing of spirit were vigorous exercises, the ultimate purpose of which was the linking of oneself to "true emptiness." Activity blended with passivity in his prescription for a way of life. The aikidōka never aggressively attacks, only responds and defends, but does so by anticipating the attack, often moving preemptively before it materializes.

After the death of its founder, the history of aikidō was shaped by a number of individuals, most of whom had been prominent among the senior students practicing in Ueshiba's dōjō. This was not always a friendly or cooperative enterprise. There were some sharp disagreements about how Ueshiba's teachings were to be interpreted and the extent to which an ongoing transformation of the founder's technique was to be considered acceptable. Rapidly, diverse schools and styles of aikidō emerged, each with distinctive emphases and characteristics. Ueshiba had forbidden competition in his dōjō, considering it antithetical to the spirit of aikidō. But at least one major style of aikidō included competition as a part of its practice, in a way similar to judō, kendō, and many schools of karate. Other styles

reincorporated into aikidō some of the early techniques that
Ueshiba had eliminated from the syllabus during the postwar
era when his art underwent its most dramatic transformation.
Many of those techniques are highly effective and deeply rooted
in the history of Japanese jūjutsu, but the effects of their application are destructive in a way that caused Ueshiba to regard
them as morally problematic.

By the end of the twentieth century, there were more than a
million practitioners of aikidō, in countries all over the world.
Even during Ueshiba's lifetime, the vast majority of visitors or
students in his dōjō could not accurately be identified as sharing
all of his religious commitments or as endorsing the ideology of
Ōmoto-kyō. Since that time, the cultural and religious diversity
of persons engaged in the study of aikidō has increased enor-
mously. In many instances, the spiritual aspects of the art that
were so important to its founder have been neglected or de-
emphasized by both instructors and practitioners. For these individuals, aikidō might be conceived primarily as a form of
self-defense or a relaxing type of physical exercise. In some dōjōs,
talk about cultivating and harmonizing with the power of ki is
ubiquitous; in others, there is little or no mention of it at all.

The relevance of these observations to the present discussion
should not be underestimated. The portrayal of aikidō as a spiritual discipline, supplied above, is a misleading one if it is assumed to represent accurately the practice of the art throughout
its history and worldwide. Nevertheless, there are several factors
that serve to mitigate the extent to which it is in fact misleading.
In the first place, unlike many other martial arts, aikidō does
have a historically identifiable "founder," one whose philosophy
and teachings have been recorded and whose techniques have
been preserved (even on film). This fact has supplied for aikidō
a principle of unity that many other martial arts are lacking, so
that despite the heterogeneity, the diversity among aikidō styles
and practitioners, there is also a certain commonality. That is to
say, there are certain standard exercises and techniques (torifune,

for example, or shihō-nage) that one would be likely to encounter in almost any dōjō, despite the extent to which others
have been changed or added. Moreover, even where there is virtually no instruction or conversation about the concept of ki,
there is quite commonly at least an implicit recognition of its
significance in aikidō training (although the concept itself may
be understood in ways rather different from its meaning in Asian
religious traditions).

There is a second factor that needs to be considered and one
that is of more general importance for understanding the relationship between meditation and the martial arts. This portrayal
of aikidō was intended to suggest that Ueshiba's religious and
moral philosophies are most eloquently articulated in the physical exercises and movements that constitute the practice of his
art. Of course, it has already been noted that these aspects of
aikidō have been vulnerable to change, sometimes in ways that
make a great deal of philosophical difference (as when a technique is adapted to be lethal rather than gently controlling and
protective). Still, it is quite likely that many contemporary aikidōka continue to practice these movements, and to engage in
these exercises, in ways roughly similar to what Ueshiba taught
and intended. Yet it is not the case that very many of these same
persons will be even vaguely familiar with the Shintō, Buddhist,
or Ōmoto-kyō beliefs that dramatically shaped Ueshiba's thinking. On this account, it must be concluded that the philosophy
of aikidō, insofar as it continues to be transmitted at all to suc-
ceeding generations of aikidōka, is primarily communicated in
this distinctive, embodied form. One need not have specific religious commitments or intend to pursue aikidō as a spiritual discipline in order to be transformed by its actual practice in subtle
but powerful ways. To this extent, it is possible to conceive of
aikidō as a meditative exercise even for persons who do not explicitly understand it as such.

Ōmoto-kyō is a Japanese "new religion," but its adherents
have typically understood it to be related in tangible and posi-

tive ways to not only Shintō, Buddhism, and other Asian traditions but religions like Judaism, Christianity, and Islam as well. In a similar fashion, Ueshiba understood aikidō to be a new creation that embodied the essence of traditional budō, and his thorough grounding in Japanese jūjutsu and swordsmanship has already been observed. A final question might be raised about the possible relationship between aikidō and martial arts traditions outside of Japan. In particular, it is difficult not to note certain similarities between the soft, circular blending techniques of aikidō and those of *taijiquan* and *baguazhang*, two Chinese arts rooted in ancient Daoist philosophy.

There is some speculation that Ueshiba might have been exposed to these Chinese disciplines during his two sojourns in Manchuria, the first as a soldier early in the century and the second as part of an ill-fated Ōmoto-kyō mission in 1924. Ueshiba's followers have tended to deny that he learned anything of substance from martial artists that he observed in China, that his own level of martial expertise was already so high that only the most exceptional of Chinese practitioners would have had anything of value to teach him. But this sort of claim must be evaluated with great care and seems primarily motivated by the desire to underscore Ueshiba's superiority to Chinese stylists. Precisely because of his genius and training as a martial artist, Ueshiba would likely have been attentive to any fighting style that he encountered, assessing and adapting techniques for his own purposes. In any event, there appears to be no definitive historical record of what Ueshiba observed or studied in Manchuria.

There are even more complicated questions, equally difficult to resolve, about the historical relationship between Chinese and Japanese martial arts in general. It is possible that there could be some influence of these soft internal styles on aikidō mediated through the Japanese martial tradition itself, independently of anything that Ueshiba personally learned in China. And there are very real and important historical connections between Daoism and Buddhism and between both of these and Shintō as the religious traditions that supplied aikidō and the Chinese martial arts with important philosophical resources. Such historical relations and possible lines of influence are not the present topic of concern, however. The question being pursued here concerns the extent to which certain martial arts can be conceived as forms of meditative practice and the similarity (even if not historically grounded) between specific martial styles in that regard.

TWO

Daoist Moving Meditation

Taijiquan and *baguazhang*, along with *xingyiquan*, constitute a trinity of Chinese martial arts styles that are frequently labeled as "internal" *(neijia,* or *neigong)*. The historical origins of this designation, its precise rationale, remain obscure. Practitioners of these arts tend to explain the label in terms of the general purpose of the exercises. On this account, martial arts known as "external" are intended primarily to enhance bodily strength, speed, and stamina, toughening the hands and feet, while developing the musculature. In contrast, the internal arts are devoted specifically to the task of generating *qi* (or *ch'i*, vital energy, the Chinese equivalent of the Japanese *ki*) and circulating it throughout the body. The ability to produce and then control this internal energy can be useful for fighting purposes. At the same time, the flow of qi bathes the major organ systems, cleansing joints and strengthening tendons and ligaments, so that the practice of these arts is also considered to be quite healthful.

This account is hardly unproblematic. Almost all of the Chinese martial arts identified as external are also concerned, to a greater or lesser extent in each case, with the project of storing and utilizing qi. At best, then, such a distinction would underscore a difference in emphasis between the internal and many of the external arts, not a fundamental contrast in practice or principle. As an explanation of how and why these classifications arose, the distinction may not be historically accurate, either. There is some speculation that certain arts came to be designated "internal" because it was believed that they were entirely indigenous, originating in China, as opposed to "external" styles that were imported from another culture and subsequently developed and refined by the Chinese (specifically, arts linked to Buddhism, which was imported from India).[1]

There is also difficulty in tracing the precise historical roots of the "internal" arts. The Daoist priest Zhang Sanfeng is traditionally celebrated as being the creator of taijiquan. Since Zhang is an obscure figure whose life has become shrouded in legend, this identification is far from informative. Most accounts place him in the thirteenth century of the common era, but reports of his exploits have them occurring as early as the eighth century and as late as the fifteenth. Indeed, since the legends ascribe to him the status of a Daoist "immortal," any precise fixing of his lifespan is questionable. A colorful and eccentric figure, Zhang is said in some legends to have formulated the basic elements of taijiquan after being fascinated while observing a desperate struggle between a magpie and a snake. Other stories portray him as being accomplished in the external martial arts associated with the Buddhist monks at the Shaolin temple. Not entirely satisfied with that practice, he sojourned to the Wu Dang mountains, where he was tutored by a Daoist hermit for a considerable period of time. As a result of what he learned, Zhang transformed and developed Shaolin *gongfu* into a form closely resembling the modern art of taijiquan.

The traditions surrounding baguazhang's beginnings are only slightly less mysterious, albeit of somewhat more recent origin. In almost all of the narrated events, Dong Haichuan (believed to have been born at the end of the eighteenth century) plays the leading role. Like Zhang Sanfeng, Dong has achieved legendary status in Chinese martial arts lore. Some accounts of his life have him, also like Zhang, developing the essential elements of his art as a result of experiences with Daoist monks in remote mountains. Already accomplished in various styles of martial art, Dong was impressed by the monks' Daoist method of circle-walking meditation. He blended the old styles with these methods in order to produce the earliest bagua forms.

The quest for the origins of these martial arts is a misguided one if the expectation is that a precise founder or period of formulation can somehow be established. It is likely that some of the philosophical ideas that supply the basic principles for these martial arts are quite ancient. Similarly, certain postures, movements, and breathing techniques that are distinctive of their practice may have a long and venerable history. At the same time, the assemblage of these elements into any kind of form that a contemporary observer would recognize as taijiquan or baguazhang is probably a relatively modern phenomenon. In any event, there is a scarcity of reliable data and thus very little historical certainty about the manner in which the internal arts evolved prior to the nineteenth century.

Comparable in difficulty to the task of exposing the historical roots of the internal arts is that of evaluating their modern status. Over the centuries, a number of different styles of taijiquan have evolved, most prominently, the Yang, Chen, Wu, and Sun styles. There is considerable debate about the exact relationship among the styles—questions concerning historical precedence and lines of influence. Moreover, there is significant variety within each major style, as forms have been adapted for various purposes, edited and abbreviated, or combined with the elements of other forms. The situation in baguazhang is somewhat comparable to that in aikidō. As with Ueshiba, Dong Haichuan's most accomplished students appear to have developed their own distinctive styles of this martial art after their master died. (On some accounts, Dong is reported actually to have taught them differently, adapting his instruction to each student's unique physical and personal characteristics.) Many of these styles incorporate some of the basic techniques of xingyiquan, the third Chinese internal art and one that has traditionally been practiced in conjunction with bagua. Sun Lutang, the creator of the Sun style of taijiquan, was trained extensively in all three internal arts. His bagua form displays considerable xingyi influence, and the Sun style of taijiquan freely borrows principles and techniques from both bagua and xingyi.[2]

While it is impossible to supply either a definitive account of the history of these arts or a perfectly clear sketch of their contemporary form, some general observations can be articulated that are relevant to this inquiry. Whatever other diverse influences may have combined to shape the development of taijiquan and baguazhang, it seems certain that Daoist philosophy and practice have played an especially prominent role in this regard. This is not to deny any relationship between these martial arts and the Buddhist exercises associated with the Shaolin temple, just as it would be foolish to ignore the complex interactions between Daoism and Buddhism in the history of Chinese religions. Nevertheless, Daoist ideology is relevant for the understanding of the internal arts in a more decisive way than it is for other Chinese martial practices. Moreover, even if its actual shaping influence on the development of these arts has been overestimated, Daoism has become crucial in modern times for the self-understanding of many taiji and bagua practitioners.

Without denying their identity as fighting arts, it is important to observe that taijiquan and baguazhang are perceived as spiritual exercises to a greater extent than most other classical or contemporary martial disciplines. Indeed, the taiji individual form is very likely the one activity most frequently characterized by both scholars and practitioners as a type of "moving meditation." Bagua circle-walking, although less well-known and not as widely performed, especially outside of China, may be even more aptly described in this fashion, given the possibility that it has evolved from or incorporated actual Daoist meditative techniques.

The fact that both of these activities are considered to be healthful and that many more people engage in them for that reason than as preparation for combat should serve to underscore rather than to distract attention away from the observations already recorded here. A Daoist perspective precludes any sharp dichotomy between physical and spiritual phenomena. Physical health and well-being are among the purposes of spiritual exercise, longevity being considered one of the primary fruits of Daoist practice. Traditional Chinese medicine is informed by ancient philosophical ideas, many of which are fundamentally Daoist, and both meditation and the martial arts are considered to be therapeutic in a way comparable to the use of herbal medicines and acupuncture.[3]

Taijiquan (popularly known in the West as tai chi chuan) is probably the most widely practiced martial art in the world, the irony being, once again, that a relatively small minority of its practitioners understand its martial significance or pursue it for purposes of self-defense. Although there is significant evidence to suggest that its techniques can be highly effective in combat, the amount of skill required in order to achieve such an effect is substantially greater than that required for the successful employment of many other martial arts techniques. This has something to do with the softness and subtlety of movements in taijiquan, the particular fighting strategy that those movements embody. Typically performed slowly, with an emphasis on gentleness and relaxation, such movements, for most uninformed observers, are difficult even to recognize as combat techniques.

Quan does literally mean "fist," indicating that taijiquan is a form of Chinese boxing. *Taiji* designates a fundamental metaphysical and cosmological principle, the "grand ultimate" from which all things originate and that itself emerges from the primordial emptiness *(wuji)*. "Tai-Chi is born of Wu-Chi. It is the origin of dynamic and static states and the mother of *Yin* and *Yang*. If they move, they separate. If they remain static, they combine."[4] *Taiji* can also be translated as "supreme pole," here signifying the cosmic ridge pole or axis around which everything in the universe is organized and revolves. The relaxed but perfectly erect posture of the taiji practitioner is ideally a representation of this cosmic phenomenon. With feet firmly rooted in the earth, weight sunken, shoulders down, and head gently stretched upward much like a puppet on a string, all the movements of the form originate from and are arranged around a stable, central axis.

The entire taiji curriculum includes the individual form, the pushing-hands exercise, a two-person sparring set, free sparring, and various weapon forms, most notably those designed for the sword. Yet a great many students of taijiquan never explore the art beyond the practice of the individual form. At a bare minimum, one could argue, some experimentation with pushing hands would seem to be an essential prerequisite for understanding its martial applications. Of course, the analysis here will suggest that this conclusion is most relevant to a conception of taijiquan that emphasizes its application as a martial art to situations of physical combat between persons. And the same analysis will reveal that such a conception is too narrow and thus inadequate for present philosophical purposes. (Nevertheless, pushing hands is a potentially valuable spiritual discipline, comparable to some of the two-person exercises performed by aikidōka, and its significance will be explored below.)

Talk about vital energy (qi), or about the essential complementarity of opposites in nature (yin/yang), is certainly not limited to Daoist discourse. These are ancient ideas with an influence that cuts across the boundaries, often blurred, between Chinese religious traditions. They are important ingredients of the Daoist perspective, however, and indispensable for understanding the internal martial arts. In the practice of taijiquan, for example, it is frequently observed that the mind moves the qi, while the qi moves the body. "The mind leads the *ch'i*, and the whole body moves as one. In movement everything moves; in stillness, all is still."[5] If awareness is focused narrowly on the physical extremities, then the arms and legs, hands and feet, will act as isolated units. When the mind attends to the continuous circulation of qi throughout the body, physical gestures become soft and flowing "and the whole body moves as one."

This emphasis on continuous movement is important in the practice of taijiquan. From the beginning of the form to its conclusion, there should be no stopping, not even brief pauses at certain points to mark the transition from one posture to another. Somewhat paradoxically, the achievement of a perfect continuity in movement is to be perceived as the simultaneous realization of a meditative tranquility, a peaceful stillness-in-motion that constitutes one of the loftiest goals of taiji practice. "*Yin* and *yang* must complement each other, as moving back and forth we shift and change. The *ch'i* is aroused with the changing power relationship, and the spirit is held within. Movement arises from stillness, but even in movement there is stillness."[6]

Just as these movements are soft, slow, and continuous, so, too, is the breathing of the taiji practitioner. The goal of the exercise is to supply an affirmative answer to the ancient question posed by the author of the Daoist classic *Dao de jing:* "In concentrating your breath and making it soft—can you make it like that of a child?"[7] This brief question exposes a variety of elements essential to the ideology of the internal martial arts, and especially to taijiquan. In the first place, the latter is a discipline of concentration—as with all meditation, a practice of attention. Initially, this is an attending to breath and breathing, to the power of qi as it first sinks to the *dan tian* (the Chinese term comparable to *hara* in Japanese), then, from that point of origin, as it travels freely through various channels, or "meridians," within the body.[8] Surprisingly, this focusing on internal processes becomes a powerful method for cultivating awareness of what lies beyond the self, a skill in "listening" and thus in interpreting the energy and intentions of other persons. Such a skill has both a spiritual and a martial significance; it can be (and later will be) analyzed from the perspective of a theory of semiotic.

The question from the *Dao de jing* explicates the desired quality of "softness" in breathing with a crucial simile: the breath should be "like that of a child." Similarly, Jesus told his disciples to become like little children; unless they did so, he said, they could not enter the kingdom of heaven.[9] But both the Daoist prescription and Jesus' admonition require careful analysis; after all, in neither tradition is every quality possessed by a child regarded as spiritually felicitous.

For the Daoist, the most literal surface reading of the question suggests that a person's breathing should mechanically resemble that of a child. It should be abdominal breathing, effected by the movement of the diaphragm—soft, regular, and comfortable as an infant's or that of a person restfully sleeping. The labored sigh of sadness or fatigue, the huff and puff of anger or exasperation, are forms of learned behavior. The natural breathing and posture of a child are exemplary; they devolve only gradually under the pressures and anxieties of later childhood, adolescence, and adulthood. The image of the child as a model both for the Daoist and for the martial artist is richer, however, than any purely mechanical talk about breathing could reveal. The *Dao de jing* develops the image in other passages, in fact, in ways that directly allude to its martial significance: "He who is filled with Virtue is like a newborn child. Wasps and serpents will not sting him; Wild beasts will not pounce upon him; He will not be attacked by birds of prey. His bones are soft; his muscles weak, But his grip is firm."[10] Here is a distinctively Daoist concept of power as consisting in virtue *(de)*. What makes it distinctive, however, is not just the connection between virtue and power (Confucianists also would affirm such a link), but rather the precise manner in which virtue (and thus, power) is portrayed. Its essence is gentleness; it is a disposition to yield. There is a vital power in weakness. Again from the *Dao de jing:* "A man is born gentle and weak. At his death he is hard and stiff. Green plants are tender and filled with sap. At their death they are withered and dry. Therefore the stiff and unbending is the disciple of death. The gentle and yielding is the disciple of life."[11]

The strategy of taijiquan is to embody such a power in physical postures and movements. Punches, pushes, or kicks, whether imagined by the practitioner of the form or actually experienced in taiji sparring, are never to be greeted with resistance or answered with force. The goal of taiji training is to cultivate a disposition of softness in movement so that an attacker encounters only emptiness and is consequently neutralized. This effect is achieved because the skilled practitioner gives such an opponent, quite literally, nothing to work with. "When the opponent brings pressure on one's left side, that side should be empty; this principle holds for the right side also. When he pushes upward or downward against one, he should feel as if encountering nothingness."[12]

A forceful, violent response offers the aggressor an opportunity to control the person attacked, just as when holding a hard, rigid object (like a staff or spear) at one end, it is possible to control the entire object, even at the other extremity. By becoming "soft like a child" one is no longer vulnerable to such manipulation. This requires "unlearning" certain instinctive patterns of response to violence or aggression and developing new habits. It also presupposes the achievement of an extraordinary state of relaxation, another one of the basic goals of regular taiji practice.[13] Such relaxation makes it possible for the martial artist to deflect "a thousand pounds' momentum with the force of four ounces."

Of course, this relaxed softness is only the essential prerequisite to a successful response to aggression. Much more is required; otherwise, small infants and heavily tranquilized persons would be more or less invulnerable to harm. In the first place, the relaxed disposition enhances awareness, a sensitivity to the intentions and strategy of an attacker. Moreover, it facilitates the effective, self-controlled movement out of danger, "deflecting" and redirecting the aggressive energy. Both this awareness and such habits of movement are skills that must be developed through continuous training. Yet they are inseparable from the basic disposition that they presuppose. And even though these are not skills that an infant would possess, it is the meditative quest to "become like a child" that stimulates their development.

Consider again this ideal of "returning" to a childlike state. Most immediately, it is the recommendation of a certain posture and method of breathing for the spiritual devotee. As the pre-scribed goal of meditation, it must also surely be understood in light of the Daoist quest for longevity—for immortality.[14] Spiri-tual practice ought minimally to be healthful, optimally to result in a recovery of the vitality of youth. But the image of the child is a complex one, the return to a childlike state representing movement back toward a primordial condition, toward union with the divine mother of all beings, the Dao. This primordial reality is initially empty, an undifferentiated sea of no-thing from which all things in their difference (yin/yang) eventually emerge. Upon "returning," the devotee encounters multiple im-ages of emptiness. Not only is the ultimate source of things (wuji) a profound emptiness, but the spiritual disposition of the child is also one "empty" of the beliefs, biases, attachments, and anxieties that typically dominate the adult consciousness. In both of these respects, meditation-as-returning is a movement toward emptiness.

The practice of taijiquan displays these distinctive character-istics of Daoist spiritual exercise. The opening of the form is an embodied representation of Daoist cosmology, the differentia-tion of yin and yang from out of the primordial emptiness. The original "One" now becomes two as the feet, initially placed to-gether with heels touching, are separated with a sinking of the weight on one foot and a stepping out to the side with the other. In the resulting stance, the feet are shoulder-width apart and the weight is again evenly balanced on both legs. The body slowly sinks and then rises as arms also rise and then sink again with a settling into this stance. Yin and yang movements blend in har-mony as the form unfolds; the emptiness is not banished but persists as a stillness-in-motion, a distinctive quality of move-ment best described by terms like *soft, continuous, yielding*. The terminus of the form is a restoration of complete stillness, the uniting of all opposites in an undifferentiated unity, the arrival in the end at a posture identical to that with which the form began.

Throughout the exercise, emptiness facilitates movement. The strategy of movement in taiji involves the "emptying" of one part of the body, for example, the emptying of one leg by shifting weight onto the other as at the beginning of the form. Thus emptied, the leg can easily be relocated, the weighted leg supplying balance, a stable axis around which such movement is organized. "Double-weightedness," or the distribution of weight evenly on both legs, is considered a cardinal error in taijiquan: whatever its stability, this type of posture clearly sacrifices freedom and flexibility of movement. When occupying such a stance, a person is vulnerable to attack, in danger, quite literally, of being "caught flat-footed." The goal of the solo exercise is to achieve continuous motion so that double-weighted postures occur only at the opening of the form and with the return to perfect stillness at its conclusion.

The practice of the form, in its entirety, is a discipline of attention, and this discipline is itself one rooted in an awareness and cultivation of emptiness. It is an exercise in learning how to *listen*, in the precise sense of that word that makes it relevant not only to Daoist spirituality but to the martial arts as well. Consider the following advice from Zhuang zi (Chuang Tzu): "Don't listen with your ears, listen with your mind. No, don't listen with your mind but listen with your spirit. Listening stops with the ears, the mind stops with recognition, but spirit is empty and waits on all things. The Way gathers in emptiness alone. Emptiness is the fasting of the mind."[15]

How is the practice of taijiquan to be understood in light of Zhuang zi's remarkable instruction? In Daoist cosmology, the primordial void is itself the embodiment of a dynamic movement.[16] Qi freely circulates only in emptiness; fullness blocks, impedes, motion. In order for qi to circulate throughout the body, all obstruction must be removed. In order for the body to move in space, it must constantly be emptied, refilled, then emptied again, all accomplished with the shifting of weight and turning at the waist. Continuous movement presupposes emptiness.

At the same time, the practice of relaxed, continuous movement is a cultivation of emptiness. The body moves. The breath circulates. The mind is linked to breath and body, stopping nowhere, attaching to nothing. Each movement is a yielding, the release of one posture in order to assume another, but the latter, too, is already dissolving even before it is fully formed. As the body learns, the spirit also learns to yield, acquiring a habit of profound humility, the opposite of being stuffed with self, frozen in spiritual death. It is in this sense that taijiquan, as a form of moving meditation, can be conceived of as a "fasting of the mind."

Thus detached, thus disposed, the practitioner is able to "listen" deeply, by fastening onto nothing in particular, is able to attend to ("wait on") all things. In order to achieve this status, a person must be willing, in the words of Zheng Manqing (Cheng Man-ch'ing), to "invest in loss."

How is this manifested in human affairs? It means to yield to others, thus quashing obstinacy, egotism, and selfishness. But it is not an easy thing. To persist in the Solo Exercise amid life's busy requirements is self-humbling. In the Pushing-Hands Practice, the student must accept failure many times over in the early stages. To yield and adhere to an opponent cannot be achieved by an egotist—his ego will not tolerate the bruisings necessary before mastery comes. But here, as in life, this proximity to reality must overcome ego if one is to walk a whole man.[17]

Here the practice of taijiquan is clearly portrayed as a spiritual exercise, its primary objective being the cultivation of virtue and the conquering of selfish impulses. Now this virtue can manifest itself as a real power, the power to control others in situations where one might be threatened or attacked. Yet the root of that power can always be traced back to certain fundamental dispositions characteristic of the person who possesses it. These dispositions are related to one another, balanced with one another, in highly specific ways. The ability to acquire such dispositions and then to bring them into harmony is the essence of self-control. Once again, power consists in a virtuous self-control. Although it is most certainly a martial art, taijiquan is primarily an exercise in "self-humbling," its primary goal being to "overcome" ego.

This harmonizing of dispositions can best be described in somewhat paradoxical terms. The precise practice of a carefully choreographed form is simultaneously a movement toward the void, toward formlessness and chaos *(hun dun)*. The discipline of taijiquan involves the acquiring of specific skills, physical skills developed in the practice of certain postures and movements, all of which have application as martial techniques. At the same time, the essential discipline is the acquiring of a powerful habit of detachment, a self-emptying, the ability to wait.[18] As a meditative practice, attention is fastened on the self, on breath and body, but as the mind becomes quiet, as breath and body become soft, the practitioner is better able to attend and then respond to others. This balance is essential. Without the cultivation of emptiness, or minus the continuous influence of a habit of detachment, taijiquan is reduced to a series of physical exercises. Certain skills will be developed, including martial ones, as well as a coordination of movement, better balance, and so forth, but the result will not be the sort of radical self-transformation that is identified as the ultimate goal of taijiquan in the taiji classics and other traditional literature.

This is not to suggest that there are two entirely different ways to pursue the practice of taiji, one as a set of physical exercises, the other as a meditative discipline fostering a sense of detachment. As with aikidō, in taijiquan the relevant philosophical principles are embodied in the movements of the form. It is a type of moving meditation, rather than a spiritual discipline appended to physical training, as something alien and external to it. Nevertheless, it is certainly possible to practice the martial art with relatively little awareness of or cultivation of its spiritual dimension. This is similar to the way in which sexual activity might appropriately be called "lovemaking," because a powerful human love can be embodied in touch and gesture, in physical union. The intention and emotion are not something super-imposed on an otherwise meaningless physical form. (Meaning emerges in the dynamic relationship between a symbol and its interpreters; it is not attached to the symbol like a code.) Yet it is easy enough to imagine how such activity can become a rela-tively meaningless physical exercise or how human sexuality might become radically transformed in its significance.

Zhuang zi referred to the emptying or "fasting" of the mind as a kind of "forgetting," and Daoist meditation devoted to that end can be designated as a practice of "sitting and forgetting."[19] It is a forgetting in the sense of not clinging to anything, not even cherished beliefs and virtues, a letting go of the body, of all thoughts and perceptions, of every kind of form. If sitting med-itation ought to be understood thus, then taijiquan can be aptly described as a method of "moving and forgetting." Not only is the purpose the same, but it is visibly displayed in the form itself since one must abandon each posture before it is ever fully formed, proceeding to the next. The completion of one move-ment is already the anticipation of another; the seed or source of yang is contained within yin, and vice versa.

The ego is constituted by attachment to beliefs, thoughts, perceptions, and body, so that this exercise is strategically de-signed to result, ideally, in the overcoming of ego. Yet the con-quering of self is simultaneously the best preparation for resisting the aggression of others. Adherence to this principle is a distinc-tive feature of martial spirituality (one that has already been observed here). In taijiquan, it is perhaps most effectively illus-trated by the pushing-hands exercise. Unlike the solo form, taiji pushing hands is performed with a partner. The way in which it is performed can vary in complexity, depending on the skill and sophistication of the practitioners, but typically it begins with partners facing each other, one foot advanced and the other back, in a relaxed but stable posture. The practitioners will usu-ally be touching but not grasping each other (grasping or grabbing is another cardinal error in taijiquan for reasons that already should be obvious), often with the back of the wrist or forearm. This touching is also a listening with the body, a waiting for indications of movement.

As one partner begins to move, so does the other. If one pushes, the other empties and yields (shifting the weight back and/or turning at the waist). As one moves back, the other "sticks" and follows. The key to control is both to achieve a high level of self-control and always to maintain contact without straining or clashing. This requires the development of a lively but soft and relaxed disposition. Practitioners quickly discover that even at a level of skill where such a disposition is readily attained in the solo form, it is difficult to preserve in the pushing-hands exercise. If separation occurs, control is lost and one becomes vulnerable to attack. Pushing hands can take the form of a contest, victory consisting in one partner's ability to move or "uproot" the other. Yet it is also frequently practiced as a kind of meditative exercise with a partner, an exercise in awareness, comparable to kokyū dōsa in aikidō. The temptation is to push too hard in order to overcome the other or to retreat too rapidly in order to protect oneself. As a spiritual discipline, the practice of pushing hands is intended to help one overcome both the desire and the fear that fuel these mistakes. These emotions cloud awareness, distort perception, and by interrupting the flow of energy between partners they poison that relationship.

Zheng Manqing, in his reflections on the pushing-hand exercise, distinguished between "listening" and "interpreting energy"; the latter he considered a higher achievement than the former.[20] In listening, one is still consciously listening "for" something, anticipating movement, attempting to stick—to adhere and follow. At a more advanced level, all this is accomplished without being consciously attempted (a manifestation of *wu wei*, the Daoist principle of effortless action, or acting without action). Interpretation is unconscious and immediate, not reactive but creative. Here one shapes the encounter, actually attracts or invites the other person's energy, then blends perfectly with it so that both persons move as if one. Zheng Manqing referred to such interpretive skill, at the peak of perfection, as "receiving energy." It is a kind of waiting without any specific expectation, a way of being and doing that "gathers in emptiness alone."

Now there is also something like taiji's pushing hands, included as a part of training, in baguazhang, in addition to various two-person drills, free sparring, and some rather idiosyncratic weapons forms (several of which involve double crescent swords unique to bagua). But the heart of training in baguazhang is the circle-walking exercise. Comparable to the solo form in taiji, circle walking is the primary method in bagua for the cultivation and circulation of qi in the body. It is an exercise that enables the practitioner to develop skill in the distinctive footwork and spiraling movements of this art, movements that embody a variety of highly effective martial techniques. Finally, it is a powerful means of shaping the practitioner's attention and developing awareness, suggesting its possible links to Daoist meditation practices. The Daoist monks who may have influenced Dong Haichuan apparently engaged in a ritual activity in which they walked in circles reciting mantras, matching attention with breathing while maintaining constant motion.[21]

Baguazhang (pa kua chang) means, literally, "eight trigram palm." The label is explained, in part, by the heavy reliance in this martial art on open-handed strikes and other techniques utilizing the palms of both hands. The reference to "eight trigrams" is an indication that baguazhang (like taijiquan, in fact) borrows important philosophical resources from the ancient Chinese classic known as the *Yi Jing* (the *I Ching*, or *Book of Changes*). The trigrams consist of different configurations of broken *(yin)* or unbroken *(yang)* lines arranged in sets of three, eight sets in all. The *Yi Jing* identifies and discusses each trigram (as well as sixty-four hexagrams); each is a rich, multivalent symbol that acquires additional layers of meaning when considered in relation to the others. The work has had a significant ideological impact in the history of China on the development both of Daoism and of Confucianism. It is a somewhat peculiar text and one that has invited and sustained a great variety of interpretations. Traditionally employed as a manual of oracles (although perhaps not so frequently among Daoists, for whom fortune-telling is somewhat problematic),[22] it is also an important cosmological and metaphysical treatise, as well as an influential source of moral wisdom. It has many complex features, but it is possible to identify the work's central philosophical tenet: everything is in flux; there are patterns and there is an order in change, but everything changes. The wise person will understand this fact and try to live and move in harmony with such a world of change.

Such, too, will be the philosophy of the person who engages in the practice of bagua circle walking as a spiritual exercise. "Done to cultivate the *tao* (the way), the circling movements of Pa-kua both manifest Heaven and Earth and order and organize *yin* and *yang*. . . . When practicing Pa-kua, you walk the circle as though macrocosmically walking in the universe, affecting and being affected microcosmically by the changes inside your body."[23] Like taijiquan, but perhaps even more emphatically, the practice of bagua stresses the importance of continuous movement and constant change. The potentially devastating palm strikes that are the signature of this art must be delivered "on the run"; that is to say, baguazhang is one of the few martial arts in which students are taught to attack while maintaining constant movement. Moreover, every advance is already a withdrawal, every attack already a form of retreat. Strategically, bagua is distinguished from most other martial arts by the unconventional nature of its attacks and responses to attack, as well as by its highly evasive footwork. Its basic principles can be summarized in the formula "Move forward and withdraw; link mind and body; practice the method of constant change."[24]

The bagua circle is of no fixed size, but usually not larger than a dozen feet in diameter (experienced practitioners often reduce the size of the circle as their skill develops, performing movements at the same speed within the more confined space). Nor is there a single method of walking the circle. It can be walked with knees sharply bent, the body very low to the ground, or in a relatively upright posture. Different kinds of steps are utilized by different stylists: heel-to-toe, or stepping first on the ball of the foot, sometimes placing all parts of the foot on the ground simultaneously, walking with high knee lift or lightly skimming over the ground, and so forth. The circle can be walked very slowly, in much the same way that the taiji solo form is practiced, or very rapidly. The rapid pace is often intended to develop speed, stamina, and practical fighting skill, while the slow movements are considered more appropriate for meditation, but there are no rigid rules linking pace to particular purposes. Movement is constant, but the practitioner's attention typically is trained on a fixed point at the circle's center.

Why do these martial artists walk in circles? If their practice is in fact partially derivative, then why did their Daoist predecessors do so? It should be noted, first, that the eight trigrams are traditionally portrayed as being arranged on a circle, each trigram being assigned a specific point on the compass. In taiji, the individual form is choreographed in such a way that a practitioner rehearses eight basic postures while addressing all eight directions during the course of the exercise. In bagua, the walker moves through each point around the perimeter of the circle, executing eight distinctive "palm changes" to reverse direction, sometimes cutting across the interior of the circle from point to point. At very high levels of expertise, a practitioner can develop awareness of each symbol as it is encountered in the flow of movement, as well as visualize its relationship to the other trigrams. Since the symbols are correlated with phenomena both in nature and within the human body, at this level the practitioner is perceived as actually enacting certain cosmological processes, as well as complex internal ones.

Indeed, the natural world appears to be shaped, to a significant degree, by forces that are cyclical or circular in character. Curved shapes and rounded figures are ubiquitous in nature; straight lines and sharp angles are rare. The seasons follow one another in cyclical pattern. The sun, moon, and other heavenly bodies appear to move in circular pathways across the sky. Tornadoes and whirlpools manifest a powerful, spiraling energy, which practitioners of baguazhang will often seek to embody in their physical movements. Even in the emptiness of the primordial void, it is believed, qi circulates endlessly, just as it moves through various circuits within a healthy human body.

The concepts of macrocosm and microcosm are crucially important for understanding Daoism in general and the internal martial arts in particular. Human beings are not isolated monads with fixed essences or identities; each person is a complex system of forces, the body being likened to a "country" populated by gods and spirits, each with separate powers and purposes.[25] The Daoist ideal is effectively to "govern" this country, to harmonize these discordant internal forces. Here is a remarkably powerful image, more literal than metaphorical, of the inner self as a landscape in which conflicts can and do occur, an interior battleground. Here, also, the experience of inner peace quite clearly results from the achievement of a certain kind of self-control.

This internal realm is not isolated from the cosmos that surrounds it; rather, it is clearly affected by it. And so it is also important for one to live in harmony with nature. Causality works in both directions, however; hence, achieving internal harmony—that is, being self-restrained and peaceful—is also the most effective means of transforming the world:

Since in this way man comes to resemble heaven and earth, he is not in conflict with them. His wisdom embraces all things, and his tao brings order into the whole world; therefore, he does not err. He is active everywhere but does not let himself be carried away. He rejoices in heaven and has knowledge of fate, therefore he is free of care. He is content with his circumstances and genuine in his kindness, therefore he can practice love.[26]

It is against this sort of philosophical background that the bagua circle-walking exercise is imbued with a deep spiritual significance. Developing martial arts skills is a task secondary in importance to the disciplined work required for self-transformation. Yet the latter involves the perfecting of certain "martial" abilities as well (once again, the ability to overcome attachments, to conquer desires, and to constrain distracting egotistical impulses). Nowhere more than in the imaginatively conceived world of the Daoists is it appropriate to talk about waging a battle on an "interior battleground." The advice supplied to rulers by the *Dao de jing* can be applied to the governance of a "country" existing either without or within. In both cases, as the wisdom of the *Yi Jing* suggests, the successful ruler will be able to avoid conflict and "practice love" only to the extent that that person is "free of care," active everywhere but not "carried away" by anything. That is to say, success presupposes a habit of detachment.

One of the most influential early works on baguazhang was a book published in 1916 by Sun Lutang, who as already noted was also one of the most well-known practitioners of the art. His description of bagua explains: "It uses winding strength, flowing movements, and the mutual interchange of positive and negative elements. When you are finished, then you know that change occurs in everything big or small."[27] Sun's philosophizing about the deeper meaning of bagua is formulated in utterances that rival Morihei Ueshiba's for vagueness (no doubt appropriately since the Daoist classics teach that the Dao itself is dark and vague and best described "without words"). The vagueness notwithstanding, his words indicate clearly that the spiritual discipline of bagua is to be regarded as a "fasting of the mind"; it is a form of meditation-as-returning and so requires a continuous embracing of emptiness. "Practice the Spirit Return-

ing to Emptiness. Smash the emptiness and escape to the real
body which is everlasting and incorruptible. Therefore what is
holy and cannot be known is called spiritual. Advance to where
both the form and spirit are mysterious. A place where the Dao
and the spirit come together."[28]

Here is a mysterious unity of "form and spirit," a profound
stillness realized in the midst of swirling motion and a movement stirring in the very heart of emptiness. As Sun Lutang
struggles to explain the essence of bagua, the meaning of this
"spirit returning to emptiness," he invokes the language of
paradox:

The idea is to store up Spirit. The outer forms of the body, hands, and
feet move at the command of the will. After a while, the body, *ch'i*,
and strength are transformed and feel like nothing. In truth, it is only
the idea of emptiness. Each time when there is stillness in the center
of movement, the body moves and I don't know it is moving. Then,
not-knowing comes into being. . . . Then you can function without
seeing and yet be orderly. Not moving and yet transforming. Not doing and yet complete. You arrive at a state of: "Fist, no fist; Mind, no
mind; No form, no shape; No me, no you." When you practice 'Spirit
Returns to Emptiness,' the spirit transforms unfathomably. It is a
mysterious Daoist achievement.[29]

It is important to take the "mysterious" quality of this
achievement seriously and not rush to reduce it to simple, ana-
lytic terms. The mystery always begins with form and the form itself can be described in minute detail. In the early stages of
practice, the matter may begin and end with form, properly or
poorly executed. Yet Sun Lutang was describing an experience
that occurs only "after a while," and it is that explanatory task
that elicits paradox. The spirit *(shen)* that transcends form is
achieved through form and not apart from it. It is more than the
mere perfection of form, but the form itself is not irrelevant. One
does all things as if not doing them (one is never "carried away"
by them). Attention is directed to the activity, but since the ac-

tivity is one of continuous movement, attention cannot rest there. This refusal to rest anywhere, this asceticism of attention, is the heart of the practice. It is the means by which the physical exercises of a martial art become transformed into spiritual practice or moving meditation.

All things run their course and pass away in time, but from this Daoist perspective time is not the enemy. To move gracefully with time and in time is not to be swept away to destruction but rather to return to the One. The discipline of "fasting and forgetting" is pursued for the purpose of returning. It involves the guiding and control of energies within the self *(dao yin)* toward that end. Whatever threatens this process is the true enemy that must be overcome. The martial language is not metaphor here. The combat is real and has real consequences. The fighting techniques embedded in the taiji form and the bagua circle-walking exercise can be quite effective, even devastatingly so. But the primary weapon wielded by practitioners of these internal arts is the power and quality of their *attention*. That power consists in a certain kind of virtue *(de)*. Although the integrity of this virtue can be challenged from without, the greatest threat of violence against it lies within the self. Here the inner/outer distinction is imperfect because the self maps the cosmos and through self-victory one "brings order into the whole world."

In the execution of its techniques, aikidō seems closer to the rapid footwork and constantly circling movements of baguazhang than to any other martial art. Both arts are essentially evasive in strategy, as direct confrontations evaporate with the sudden appearance, alongside or even behind the attacker, of the person attacked. And both adhere to a circular logic: all movement traces at least part of a circle; the body constantly spirals and turns. Theoretically, assaulting a person skilled in aikidō or baguazhang should be like trying to embrace a spinning top.

Taijiquan shares basic principles and techniques with both aikidō and bagua. Its movements, too, are characteristically soft and circular, but here the softness is emphasized more and, compared with most styles of the other two arts, strict adherence to spherical motion perhaps emphasized less. In taiji pushing hands, as in aikidō, one should respond to an attack by receiving and transforming the aggressive energy in much the same way that a revolving door reacts when pushed. The more forceful and violent the pushing, the more rapidly the attacker moves. The trajectory of this movement, however, is not over or through the person attacked but harmlessly around the stable center provided by that person for the encounter. Here, the image of a revolving door is somewhat hyperbolic; any ordinary, hinged door can also illustrate the point. If tightly locked or nailed shut the door will not open when touched, and in order to pass through one likely has to break it down. If, on the other hand, the door is not thus fastened, when pushed (or pulled) it yields and freely turns on its hinges. What is important is that it not be *fastened*. In the martial arts, freedom of movement—physical but also spiritual freedom—is facilitated by a quality of detachment. It is a surrendering of control over "this thing here," an abandoning also of the illusion of control and a willingness to "invest in loss" that results in mastery.

These similarities in physical technique are relevant to the present discussion only to the extent that philosophical principles can be effectively embodied in physical movement. The assumption that this is so is the basic rationale for conceiving of these martial arts as forms of moving meditation. Such an assumption is of course contestable: the very idea of "moving meditation," although it is quite commonly featured in portrayals of the internal martial disciplines, is not one that everybody would agree is even coherent.[30] It is important to recognize that the assumption might have to be argued—that such a conception of the martial arts might have to be defended. The rejection of such an idea is grounded in the following type of contrast: Meditation involves the achievement of a certain stillness, a quieting and emptying of the mind, the realization of "no-mind."

The forms practiced by martial artists, on the other hand, require continuous movement, while simultaneously *attending* to and controlling that movement. In that respect, the two kinds of practice are "antithetical."

The creation of such a contrast seems problematic for two reasons. In the first place, *meditation* is a rather vague term denoting a great diversity of practices. This is not to suggest that the struggle to achieve some precision in the use of the term is of no scholarly value. The word becomes meaningless if *any* kind of cognitive activity (or nonactivity) can be regarded accurately as "meditative." More specifically, the term seems to designate the disciplined exercise of attention for purposes of self-transformation, an exercise requiring the achievement of a certain quality of attention. Nevertheless, attention can be exercised in various ways and directed toward diverse objects. In many respects, Daoist mediation differs significantly from Buddhist meditation. And neither closely resembles Ignatian meditation in the Christian tradition. Of course, the philosopher of religion ought to be sensitive to continuities among diverse styles of meditative practice. Still, the simple definition that the contrast above presupposes is unnecessarily restrictive.

Furthermore, even employing this sort of definition, the alleged contrast seems false, or at least not obviously true. Both Ueshiba and the traditional masters of the Chinese internal styles did, in fact, conceive of meditation as involving an "emptying of the mind" and the achievement of a certain stillness. From their perspective, mindful performance of a series of physical movements is not antithetical to this process; rather, it facilitates it. Attending to continuous movement of body and breath can be a strategy for emptying the mind, a type of mental "fasting," as described above. Although the body constantly moves, even at a rudimentary level one must be able to organize movement around a stable center. And no one can claim serious achievement in these martial arts without the attainment of a more profound "stillness-in-motion." This sort of talk may seem

paradoxical to someone who has not experienced the phenomenon being described, but such talk is ubiquitous in the literature devoted to these martial practices.

Ueshiba and the Chinese internal stylists would agree that
both meditation and the martial arts are disciplines devoted primarily to the cultivation of ki, or qi. In their philosophies, this
concept provides the link between breath/body and spirit. The
cultivation and control of this vital energy is the key to defending oneself, whether against the attack of another person or the
internal threat that manifests itself in the form of physical ill-
ness or psychic distraction. Methods of visualizing and circulating
qi/ki are numerous and often baroque in their details; this is
true both in Daoism and in the idiosyncratic form of Shintō
practiced by Ueshiba. But here, too, one can discover common
themes and elements. For example, certain forms of breathing/
chanting meditation in the history of Daoism resemble the
kotodama ritual to which Ueshiba was assiduously devoted.[31]
Moreover, both in aikidō (torifune) and in baguazhang (circle
walking), one can observe the creative adaptation of specific religious exercises for the purpose of martial training.[32]

There is of course a fundamental contrast between aikidō
and the two Chinese martial arts under discussion. As already explained, aikidō is an essentially interactive and interpersonal
activity. The bulk of its practice occurs on the mats with a partner—sometimes with several partners, as in randori. Although
there are weapons kata and solo exercises, it is difficult to train in
aikidō by oneself: it is an inherently social discipline, with a distinctively ethical dimension. Taijiquan and baguazhang, on the
other hand, emphasize the practice of individual forms. Especially in the case of taiji, a significant number of practitioners
confine themselves entirely to this exercise, perhaps moving
alongside and in unison with other practitioners, but never
touching or interacting with them as in the aikidō dōjō.

The potential significance of this contrast should not be ignored. These are distinctive martial arts, marked by different

techniques and each characterized by peculiar emphases. Working hands on with a partner provides a type of training that cannot be perfectly reproduced in a solo exercise. Moreover, there is a precision and a meditative quality of movement, one could claim, that can only be perfected in an individual form, even if it is later extended in application to situations of encounter and interaction. Each type of practice has its purpose, advantages, and limitations.

That said, neither should the differences be exaggerated. There are ways to soften the contrasts. Traditional teaching of the Chinese martial arts does emphasize pushing hands, sparring, and other interactive exercises in ways comparable to aikidō, and different from the manner in which these disciplines are taught in a typical modern (and Western) context. Moreover, recall the seriousness with which a traditional Daoist perspective regards the individual form as always already constituting a social practice. This is not just superficially true in the sense that one might be encouraged to envision imaginary combatants as one executes the form; it is a more radical truth being affirmed about the individual as a "society" in microcosm, embodying forces and factions, sometimes in harmony but often in conflict. The symbolic relationship between this inner world and the cosmos, between the inner self and its outer environment, exposes a real continuity between the two realms. That is precisely why and how the internal work of *qi gong (ch'i kung)* can prove to be effective in the world—can be socially and politically transformative.

Such a perspective lays the groundwork for an explanation of how some forms of religious meditation can be martial in character, representing *preparation* for actual engagement in a kind of spiritual conflict. Like the Daoists (and to some extent influenced by them) Ueshiba articulated a similar perspective. This is related to the issue of whether or not it is legitimate to regard certain martial practices as forms of meditation, but it is also different from it. Even if such a view is warranted, it does not automatically hold true that meditation *as* meditation has any sort of martial function or characteristics. Perhaps techniques no longer useful for fighting can be employed by religious devotees for purposes of spiritual discipline. These need not be martial purposes. What, then, exactly is required in order to justify or even make sense of discourse about "spiritual combat"?

THREE

Yoga/Zen/Jihad

The Bhagavad Gita is part of the sacred literature of Hinduism, for many modern Hindus the most significant part and for many non-Hindus the primary lens through which they have come to perceive that tradition. It is a poetic narrative that constitutes a fragment of a much longer story, the great Indian epic known as the Mahabharata. The poem dramatizes the conversation between a noble warrior, Arjuna, and his charioteer, Krishna. The existential crisis that precipitates the discussion is Arjuna's experience of weakness of will as he prepares to engage in combat. Arjuna is reluctant to do battle with an army that includes many of his own kinfolk, a battle that represents the culmination of a longstanding feud between rival families. Krishna (who reveals his divine nature to Arjuna in a spectacular theophany in the story's eleventh chapter) counsels the warrior about why he must overcome his doubts and take up the fight—advice that has become perhaps the most influential piece of spiritual wisdom in the history of Hinduism.

To affirm the historical impact of the Bhagavad Gita is not to conclude that there has ever been a simple consensus about how it ought to be understood. In fact, its enduring influence may be explained in part by the way in which the poem has inspired so many different and often conflicting interpretations.[1] The purpose of the present discussion is not to argue for the superiority of one interpretation over others; rather, it is intended to provide a brief sketch of how the discipline of yoga might be conceived in the martial terms supplied by the Bhagavad Gita. The narrative begins with a crisis of volition, but as it draws to a conclusion Arjuna is firmly resolved to enter into combat. How might one evaluate the spiritual significance of this transformation?

At the time when the Bhagavad Gita was produced (approximately the third century B.C.E.), one of its primary purposes must have been to underscore the importance of each person fulfilling their social responsibilities *(dharma)*. As a member of the warrior caste, it is Arjuna's *duty* to fight, and the war in which he is about to engage is in fact a just war; that is, from the perspective supplied by the larger narrative, his cause is a righteous one. In encouraging Arjuna, Krishna appeals directly to these facts, admonishing him to perform the duties required by his station in life and warning that failure to do so will make him appear cowardly and result in his humiliation. If the rationale for fighting had been restricted to such arguments, however, the Bhagavad Gita would clearly never have acquired its present status as a spiritual classic.

In addition to the arguments about social responsibility and the duties associated with caste, Lord Krishna supplies additional reasons for Arjuna to act that are explicitly religious in character. One reason is that a reluctance to fight betrays a false understanding of the nature of the self and its relationship to the ultimate reality *(Brahman)*. In truth, Krishna explains, there is only one reality, one supreme self that has always existed and can never die or cease to exist. This self is not killed when the body is killed. All contingent things come and go, but their true nature persists unaltered. So Arjuna can enter the battle unconcerned about the necessity of killing others and without any cause for "grieving" afterwards.[2] He is like an actor in the theater, anxious about playing his role because of a mistakenly exaggerated idea about the importance of his behavior on stage.

In another theological argument, not unrelated to this metaphysical one about the self's true nature, Krishna articulates a theory of action conceived as yoga, or self-discipline. From this viewpoint, even the activity of war can be transformed into a spiritual exercise. In a lengthy discourse in chapter 2 and then in additional instructions throughout the poem, Krishna expounds on the meaning of yoga in order to shed light on Arjuna's predicament. He repeatedly affirms one fundamental prescription: Arjuna must act, but he must act calmly, with self-restraint, and in a way that is free from desire: "Work alone is your proper business, never the fruits it may produce: let not your motive be the fruits of works nor your attachment to mere worklessness. Stand fast in Yoga, surrendering attachment; in success and failure be the same and then get busy with your works. Yoga means 'sameness-and-indifference.'"[3]

Renouncing the fruits of action without renouncing action itself is the key strategy that Krishna recommends to Arjuna. In order to execute this strategy, he must cultivate an equanimity of spirit grounded in the awareness of his true nature as enduring; since it is eternally self-same, it cannot be vulnerable to changing circumstances. When he is able to stand "motionless and still, immovable in enstasy," Arjuna will have achieved the goal of yogic discipline, a perfect "skill in performing works."[4] The concept of enstasy (samādhau) employed here refers to a concentrated state of inner peace, in contrast to the "ecstatic" rupturing of the boundaries of the self in the identification with something beyond it.[5] This peace can be maintained in the midst of vigorous action (comparable, in some ways, to the realization of "stillness-in-motion" in Chinese internal boxing). Desire drives a person either to renounce action or to be enslaved to the fruits of action. The path to peace is through the rigorous control of desire. Here, the meaning of yoga has been defined aptly but rather vaguely in terms of the ideal of "sameness-and-indifference." As indicated, this concept of sameness has metaphysical implications pertaining to the divine nature. More pragmatically, it connotes habits of feeling and behavior born of indifference to the fruits of action and to external contingencies. One is disposed toward pain and pleasure, toward success and failure, in exactly the "same" fashion.

The challenge of reducing the vagueness associated with the word *yoga* is intensified by an awareness that it has been employed historically to designate almost every kind of spiritual exercise in the Hindu tradition. In fact, its usage extends beyond the Hindu tradition: one can also speak of Indian schools of Buddhist yoga or Jain yoga. (Further afield, but adding to the potential confusion, talk about "Daoist yoga" is also relatively commonplace.) Nevertheless, there is a classical subtradition within Hinduism associated with the name of Patañjali and the terse instruction provided in his Yoga Sutras. The precise dating of these writings and the fixing of the authorship are issues that have precipitated considerable scholarly discussion and debate; but the historical details about the text assume less importance if one believes, as most scholars do, that the type of meditation described in the text is very ancient indeed and much older than the Yoga Sutras themselves.

The root meaning of *yoga* in the Sanskrit is "to bind together"—"to yoke." There is both an aptness and an irony in the use of such a term to designate these Hindu spiritual practices. It is appropriate because to succeed in the practice is effectively to bind oneself to the ultimate reality, to embrace one's true nature *(ātman)*. The irony in such usage consists in the fact that this can be accomplished only to the degree that one also succeeds in detaching oneself from worldly desire and all its progeny. So yoga is an unbinding and a letting-go, a path to freedom as self-mastery; yet it is also a binding of oneself to the truth, in its theistic versions, a powerful, passionate form of loving devotion to God.

Both the project of detachment and the final goal of union with the divine presuppose the skillful control by the self of its powers of attention. The second of Patañjali's sūtras, in fact, defines yoga as the control or "suppression of the modifications of the mind."[6] The essence of spiritual exercise is firmly to fix one's attention on what matters most. This agenda is constantly being interrupted by a great variety of perceptions, feelings, thoughts, and desires that pollute consciousness as *distractions.* Yoga is the disciplined suppression and control of such distractions or "modifications of the mind." It involves the persistent attempt, by "practice and detachment" (twelfth sūtra) to achieve a calm state of concentrated attention *(samprajñāta-samādhi)* as a prelude to an even more profoundly peaceful state in which all thought is "arrested" *(nirodha)* and the mind becomes empty. This emptiness represents a condition of liberation as well as a heightened form of religious awareness.

The first part of the Yoga Sutras describes the type of concentration (quality of mind) that can be attained in meditation, as well as the numerous obstacles (distractions) that threaten to undermine this task. The goal is not the achievement of some labile condition. Real progress consists in the development of powerful habits of mind, the formation of distinctive traits of character. Yoga is intended for the purpose of dramatic self-transformation, not for the sparking of flashes of insight or of powerful but transitory experiences. In the second part of Patañjali's text, the basic methods designed to achieve such transformation are described—the eight "limbs" of yoga:[7] restraint from evil *(yama),* observances *(niyamas),* posture *(āsana),* regulation of breath *(prānāyāma),* withdrawal of the senses *(pratyāhāra),* fixity of mind *(dhāranā),* meditation *(dhyāna),* and absorption in the ātman *(samādhi).*

The first two limbs comprise the moral and ascetic aspects of spiritual practice: restraint from evildoing (such as stealing, lying, and harming others) and the observance of rules of purity, self-mortification, and devotion to study and to God. The last three limbs are identified here in the second part of the sutras but discussed only in the third part, where the "powers" of yoga associated with various levels of concentration are specified and briefly described. None of these levels of concentration can be attained without a complete mastery of the mind over the senses, a detachment from and refusal to be controlled by the objects of sense experience (the fifth limb).

From the perspective established in the earlier discussions of aikidō, taijiquan, and baguazhang, it is interesting to note the importance in yoga both of posture and of regulated breathing, the third and fourth limbs. These postures are essentially static, so that yoga, unlike the other disciplines, should not be classified as a type of "moving meditation." Nevertheless, they all share one basic assumption: to engage in spiritual exercise requires careful attention to the body and bodily dispositions. Certain distinctive habits of posture and of breathing not only signify but also help to engender a spiritually felicitous condition. The concept of *prāna* in yoga is comparable to that of qi/ki in the internal martial arts. A vital energy that circulates throughout the body, it can be facilitated by posture, while also being regulated by complex breathing exercises and various forms of meditation. The practitioner of yoga perceives the body as a laboratory in which to conduct rigorous experiments in the pursuit of religious insight and self-transformation.

Yoga is not traditionally thought of as a martial art in the conventional sense; the physical exercises that are a part of training in yoga have no practical application as fighting techniques. Nevertheless, the martial flavor of this training is discernible enough to merit consideration. The Indian deity Shiva, who Hindus often associate with the promotion of martial virtue, is also considered to be the "patron of all yogis, precisely because yoga is an arduous undertaking, a path strewn with obstacles and one that demands heroic fortitude on the part of the adept who follows it."[8] Consider also the history of usage in India of the word *kratu*, originally identified with the overwhelming power of great warriors, including the god Indra, but gradually acquiring an extended meaning so that it could later refer to the moral force embodied in a person of great piety—to the spiritual power of the religious devotee.[9]

The concept of yoga in the Bhagavad Gita is not identical to the one employed in the classical tradition summarized by the aphorisms of Patañjali; however, there is considerable continuity of meaning between the two, as exemplified in the image of the yogi appearing at the end of chapter 5 of the Gita: "All contact with things outside he puts away, fixing his gaze between the eyebrows; inward and outward breaths he makes the same as they pass up and down the nostrils. With senses, mind, and soul restrained, the silent sage, on deliverance intent, who has forever banished fear, anger, and desire, is truly liberated."[10]

Most of the discourse about yoga in the poem focuses on three great paths to liberation: *jñāna-yoga* (the way of knowledge), *karma-yoga* (the way of action), and *bhakti-yoga* (the way of loving devotion). Although each way is distinctive, each is also governed by the same essential logic of self-forgetfulness (as in Daoism, the "forgetting" of egoistic desires and attachments in order to discover one's true nature). The exhortation to perform "works" in a spirit of detachment, delivered by Krishna to Arjuna in chapter 2, encapsulates the basic philosophy of karmayoga. And there is significant emphasis in the text on the liberating power of religious knowledge as well—for example, in Krishna's speech at the beginning of chapter 13.

It is bhakti, however, that plays the most prominent role in the Bhagavad Gita's teachings about yoga (bhakti is given relatively minor status in the philosophy of Patañjali). Consider Krishna's final instruction and promise: "Bear Me in mind, love Me and worship Me, sacrifice, prostrate yourself to Me: so will you come to Me, I promise you truly, for you are dear to Me. Give up all things of law, turn to Me, your only refuge, for I will deliver you from all evils; have no care."[11] Bhakti, the path of devotion, is not being proposed here as an alternative to meditative exercise; rather, the deity is now revealed as the most appropriate object of meditation, the ideal focus of loving attention.

What, then, is the relevance of Krishna's teaching to a consideration of the relationship between meditation and the martial arts? Its primary significance is not that he appeals to ideas associated with the meditative discipline of yoga in order to convince Arjuna to engage his enemies and fight. Instead, the outbreak of war between rival clans is only the occasion for a conversation that reveals the face of Arjuna's true enemy. That conversation occurs on a field of battle, with the despondent warrior slumped in his chariot as it sits in an empty space between the two opposing armies; but the real battleground lies within himself. When, in chapter 3, a still-reluctant Arjuna inquires what it is that drives a person to do evil things, sometimes unwillingly, Lord Krishna responds:

Desire it is: Anger it is—arising from the constituent of Passion—all devouring, mightily wicked, know that this is your enemy on earth. As fire is swathed in smoke, as a mirror is fouled by grime, as an embryo is all covered up by the membrane envelope, so is this world obscured by that. This is the wise man's eternal foe; by this is wisdom overcast, whatever form it takes, a fire insatiable. Sense, mind, and soul, they say, are the places where it lurks; through these it smothers wisdom, fooling the embodied self. Therefore restrain the senses first: strike down this evil thing!—destroyer alike of what we learn from holy books and what we learn from life. . . . Vanquish the enemy, Arjuna! Swift is he to change his form, and hard is he to conquer.[12]

As before, Krishna enjoins Arjuna to fight. Yet now that call to battle has taken on a radically new meaning. Here the enemy is identified as a desire that clouds everything as smoke obscures fire, overwhelming the senses and laying waste to mind and soul. The weapon for resisting it is not the archer's bow that Arjuna carries in his chariot but the discipline of yoga that Krishna commends to him—the method of "sameness-and-indifference."

While already regarded as Hindu scripture and as a classic work of Indian literature, the Bhagavad Gita acquired a prestige and significance during the twentieth century far greater than what it had enjoyed previously.[13] A number of reasons might be invoked to explain its modern prominence, among them Indian nationalism and the rise of a militant Hinduism. That is to say, it has been a fairly common strategy to appeal to the Bhagavad Gita for the ideological defense of a martial activism. Such an activism was advocated, for example, in the summons of support for a military overthrow of British rule early in the twentieth century, and it has been displayed in the modern history of violent conflicts between Hindus and Muslims. It is interesting to note, then, how the Indian philosopher and statesman Mahatma Gandhi also ascribed to this text an extraordinary importance, while invoking it in defense of his radical doctrine of nonviolence.[14]

Gandhi agreed that the teachings of the Bhagavad Gita embody a call to action, but he rejected the notion that any consistent reading of the text would interpret this as a recommendation of violent behavior. "Violence is simply not possible," Gandhi argued, "unless one is driven by anger, by ignorant love and by hatred." These are precisely the passions that the practitioner of yoga, as described in the Bhagavad Gita, seeks to bring under control and then to eradicate. The argument for nonviolence by no means undermines the appropriateness of martial images in Krishna's discourse. In fact, Gandhi echoes that manner of speech when he proclaims that "The battle-field is our body. The poet-seer, who knows from experience the problems of life, has given a faithful account of the conflict which is eternally going on within us."

Gandhi contended that it is more appropriate for a person "who has not yet awakened to the truth of non-violence" to react with violence in the confrontation with evil than to respond in a cowardly fashion. There is real evil in the world, just as the threat of evil lurks within each one of us. To advocate a nonviolence nourished by spiritual discipline is not to deny the importance of a given conflict or abdicate the responsibility to fight. For Gandhi, nonviolence was a form of power ("soul power"), a heroic form of resistance to evil and injustice. Here is another example of a martial spirituality, and again the self is the primary locus of conflict; again, too, the spiritual victories won there generate a kind of power manifested as virtuous self-control. To wield that power in the world, to act courageously when confronted with evil, requires and results in dramatically transformed strategies of combat and resistance. From Krishna and Laozi (Lao-tzu) to Gandhi and Ueshiba, that insight remains a standard feature of the sort of perspective being explored here.

No tradition of religious meditation has been linked more consistently to the martial arts than Zen Buddhism, despite the fact that a doctrine of nonviolence (ahimsā) is as fundamental to Buddhist ideology as it was to Gandhi's Hinduism. This connection may be almost as ancient as Zen Buddhism itself. An Indian sage, Bodhidharma, is believed to have carried Chan, or Zen, Buddhism to China, perhaps in the fifth or sixth century of the common era. Although there is no real certainty about the precise historical facts, legend credits Bodhidharma with having introduced martial exercises into the training regimen of Chinese Buddhist monks at the Shaolin temple. The stories about him suggest that Bodhidharma was dismayed by the monks' inability to endure the prolonged rigors of Buddhist meditative practice. The physical exercises associated with the Shaolin martial arts were intended to facilitate spiritual exercise, sharpening awareness, and developing powers of concentration.

Even if the legend contains only a fragment of the truth, Bodhidharma represents a Buddhist tradition with roots that already ran deep in the history of India. The creative interaction between Buddhism and indigenous Chinese religions resulted in new spiritual forms, even as Chan Buddhism would later be transformed in the Japanese context as Zen. It is in this respect that Bodhidharma should be regarded as the father of Chan Buddhism. And the relationship between Buddhist meditation and the martial arts seems to have been established very early on in the history of the Chinese development of the tradition.

It is the later evolution of Zen in Japan that constitutes the primary object of inquiry here. A vast literature has been devoted to exploring the influential role of Zen Buddhism in shaping Japanese martial disciplines and ideologies.[15] These remarks will be highly selective, focusing on three specific aspects of that relationship. First, it is important to assess the emphasis that certain texts place on cultivating a state of no-mind *(mushin)* as an element of the Japanese warrior's strategy for success in combat. There is a tangible historical link between Zen Buddhist and Daoist deliberations concerning emptiness. Within Daoism, the primordial reality is characterized as being essentially indeterminate and empty; in practicing the Daoist arts, one seeks to return to such a condition. As Buddhism was introduced into the Chinese environment, Indian Buddhist reflections on the emptiness of all forms *(śūnyatā)* were inevitably reinforced and enriched by these Daoist ideas, resulting in the emergence of Chan as a distinctive perspective. Japanese Zen Buddhists later continued to elaborate on this theme and it eventually became a central ideological feature of the Japanese martial arts.

Secondly, the same texts portray the ideal Japanese warrior as someone who has learned from Zen Buddhist philosophy about the meaning of *death*. Because of this Zen insight, such a person would be fully prepared to die. And this state of preparedness would make the Zen warrior a fearless and fearsome opponent. It can be argued that religion, in many of its forms, is all about death (even as war is about life and death), about its spiritual significance, and about how life's meaning can survive the encounter with death. Zen Buddhism involves prolonged meditation on these topics, a discipline that has deeply influenced the ideology of certain Japanese martial traditions.

Finally, it was the Buddhist legacy, blended with elements of Confucianism, that creatively determined the extent to which loyalty came to be considered an essential feature of the Japanese warrior's code. There is a temptation to caricature meditative practices as being essentially private, as acts performed by religious persons "in their solitude."[16] Yet they have an inevitably public and social dimension, as the discussions of aikidō, yoga, and the Chinese internal styles have indicated. Not only are the meanings of these practices socially established and defined, they also are typically conceived as preparation for action in the world, for effective interaction with others. Martial meditation is a training to resist evil in the world. Religious meditation is frequently conceived as a kind of training for the rigors of the moral life. The social and moral aspects of spiritual discipline are vividly illustrated in the Japanese martial traditions by a pronounced emphasis on the virtue of loyalty.[17]

These three topics—by no means an exhaustive list of the ways in which Zen philosophy can be related to the ideology of the martial arts—are the features of that relationship most relevant to the present inquiry, for reasons that hopefully can be articulated in a few brief remarks. Consider again the Buddhist ideal of mushin. The word is formed by two characters in the Japanese signifying the concept of "no," or "nothing" *(mu)* combined with the idea of "mind" or "spirit" *(shin)*.[18] The Japanese pronunciation of *mu* is a transformation of the Chinese *wu*. Recall the earlier discussion of wuji, that primal nothingness in Daoist cosmology from which all determinate beings are distinguished and emerge. It is not, properly speaking, a "state of being"; rather, it is a preontological condition prior to being—a state of no-being. Correspondingly, mushin is less accurately identified as a state of mind than as "no-mind." What, then, in the practical terms required in order to design a strategy for meditation, does this concept of no-mind signify?

Here one can begin to expose the relevance of this theme to the larger set of issues under consideration. Mushin is related, as a cultivated habit of detachment, to the entire collection of beliefs, skills, and dispositions that any given person will possess. It is a vast, empty "space" wherein they are all contained.[19] It conditions them, limits their power, even occasionally dissolving and absorbing them. They acquire a special quality because of the context that it provides. Mushin is not to be regarded as a mindless state, as a trivial kind of thoughtlessness; rather, if it can be said to be anything, it is an indeterminacy that is manifested in a fluidity and flexibility of spirit. Nothing contained within this "space" can become fixed, congealed, or hardened. Mushin adds nothing to the thoughts that it contains, and mushin itself is never enslaved by those thoughts. This no-mind can possess everything and yet still remain empty.

A Chinese story is told in order to try to illustrate the quality of detachment characteristic of mushin. The story contrasts this no-mind with the condition in which a person is controlled by thoughts and feelings, rather than having mastered them.[20] In the story, a scholar cares for the son of a distant relation who has become ill while a guest in his house. The scholar is confident that he knows the proper medical treatment, administers it, and then retires to bed, awakening three times during the night to check briefly on his patient's progress, but otherwise enjoying a sound and relaxed sleep. On another occasion, the scholar's own son is staying with relatives in a remote province. A traveler from that province, upon arrival, reveals to the scholar that when he left on his journey the boy had been quite ill; consequently, the scholar endures a long, agitated, sleepless night, even though there is absolutely nothing that he can do to help his son.

This story is not intended to communicate that mushin is merely a confidence in action, or that it is the ability, in circumstances where one can do nothing useful, simply not to care. Yet there *is* a kind of confidence, as well as a certain quality of indifference, that can appropriately be included in descriptions of this state of no-mind. It is not a confidence grounded solely or even primarily in a realistic appraisal of one's level of skill for performing such action. Detachment from the consequences of action is itself the definitive skill in acting. This is the spiritual condition of being "unfettered" that Takuan Sōhō recommended to his friend as crucial, both in the martial arts and in life: "When this No-Mind has been well developed, the mind does not stop with one thing nor does it lack any one thing. It is like water overflowing and exists within itself. It appears appropriately when facing a time of need."[21]

Here is a state of indeterminacy manifesting itself as perfect freedom and plenitude. Nothing is lacking for this mind (this "no-mind") because it "does not stop with one thing" or in any particular place. From Takuan's perspective, to "stop" the mind is to precipitate a state of confusion with potentially disastrous consequences. In the martial arts, if one fixes attention on an opponent's right hand, one becomes vulnerable to an attack with the left. If focused on a threat that appears from the front, one can easily be attacked and subdued from behind. The key is to remain "completely oblivious to the hand that wields the sword," and so to abide in emptiness.

The cultivation of mushin has a broad significance that extends far beyond its providing a strategic advantage in sword fighting. Since everything in the world of sense experience is in constant flux, an attempt to "stop" the mind achieves the opposite effect of what is intended (if a swimmer in a rapidly moving stream clings to passing debris, the swimmer is caught up and swept away). "The mind of attachment arises from the stopping mind. So does the cycle of transmigration. This stopping becomes the bonds of life and death."[22] Even when not in confrontation with another warrior in a duel, the struggle with distracting thoughts and desires can have life-and-death implications.

As a practiced state of detachment, mushin is a setting of the mind on nothing in particular and so a *readiness* for whatever may appear: "By wisdom we do not mean some particular faculty or philosophy. It is the readiness of the mind that is wisdom."[23] This readiness is a habit of interpretation, since the meaning of things encountered in experience can best be discerned (rather than distorted) by a mind that is not predisposed toward any particular meaning in advance. It is useful to understand the emptiness of mushin in terms of readiness, because the latter is a positive notion, signifying a heightened awareness, a type of mindfulness. One does not achieve such a state of consciousness by trying to drive all thoughts out of the mind or to obliterate the mind's contents. Instead, in calmness one links the mind to the breath, attentive to all thoughts and feelings as they move into and out of consciousness, watching them come and go, listening to them, but never with attachment and never with any specific expectation about what will appear next. There is a certain playful quality to this mindset—the free play of images and ideas made possible by the mind's own emptiness.[24]

In the literature linking Zen philosophy to the martial arts, such play is sometimes portrayed in terms of the dialectical relationship between *isshin* and *zanshin*.[25] Isshin is a state of intense concentration, a decisive acting with "one mind" or "one spirit." With each thrust of the spear or cut of the sword, one's whole self must be committed; there can be no hesitancy or uncertainty in action. Zanshin is a broader form of awareness, a manifestation of mushin: watchful, waiting, and unattached. Rather than canceling isshin, zanshin is said to contain and condition it, even to constitute the ground of its possibility. Waiting is not pure passivity, but contains within itself the seeds of action.

This dialectic is also captured in the classical Zen talk about the cultivation of "beginner's mind." The more skillful that one becomes (in the martial arts, for example), the more important it becomes to return continuously to the perspective of the beginner. That is the only way to resist the hegemony of entrenched habits and prevent becoming enslaved by one's own polished techniques. "If your mind is empty, it is always ready for anything; it is open to everything. In the beginner's mind there are many possibilities; in the expert's mind there are few."[26]

The lack of flexibility in a mind whose thoughts are hardened or congealed must eventually result in spiritual death. The purpose of spiritual exercise is to avoid such a condition; on the other hand, what persons normally think of as death and dying themselves are not to be eschewed. Indeed, "to live in the realm of the Buddha nature means to die as a small being, moment after moment."[27] Note the distinction here between the Buddha nature and the "small being," one's finite self or ego. Of equal significance is the observation that death cannot be limited to a decisive moment in time, but rather is a continuous process. From the perspective of Zen, the self is real only in the present moment. As soon as that moment is experienced, the self that then existed is no more. Every moment is a dying, then, an irretrievable loss of self. But the continual death of the self is an extraordinary opportunity to practice detachment. To live fully in each moment but cling to none of them is the essence of freedom, a freedom from desire and the suffering that it brings.

To live the whole of life fully but not to cling to it is an extended view of what it means to be free. Takuan recalled how "at the gathering at Gridhrakuta Peak when Shakyamuni [Gautama Buddha] was about to die, he held up a single red lotus. He showed this to eighty thousand monks and every one of them remained silent. Only Kashyapa smiled."[28] For Shakyamuni, that smile was the sign of Kashyapa's enlightenment; and so it was to him that the Buddha entrusted his doctrine. What is it that Kashyapa had realized? Elsewhere, Takuan explained that "the body is like a dream. When we see this and awaken, not a trace remains. How much time is left for the looking?"[29]

In order to become thus awakened, the Zen monk Hakuin recommended that every warrior engage in persistent meditation on the "death koan": "After you are dead and cremated, where has the main character gone?" It is the fear of death that causes a warrior to be timid, hesitant, and weak when facing the enemy. That fear is eliminated by concentrating on one's "original face" or "main character," not the "small self" that dies in each moment but the Buddha nature within. No sword can touch it; no enemy can harm it. To penetrate this koan is to be transported to "the realm in which birth and death are transcended, where the place in which you stand is the Diamond indestructible, and where you have become a divine immortal, unaging and undying. The word *death* is the vital essential that the warrior must first determine for himself."[30]

The kind of self-mastery that such insight helps to produce is also the key to mastery in the martial arts. At the same time, it is a self-transformation that results in a dramatic change in the way in which one perceives the "enemy" and in the manner in which one is likely to respond. "I do not see the enemy" is how Takuan described this enlightened perspective.[31] It is not a failure to see the person right before one's very eyes who threatens harm; nor is it a refusal ever to respond to such a person with force (although such a response, if required, must be "concentrated," unmotivated either by anger or desire). Nevertheless, the mind no longer attends to such a person with hatred as the "enemy," just as it no longer attaches itself to life with desire or flees from the possibility of death with anxiety and fear. As the "small self" or ego is vanquished, the vivid distinction between "self" and "enemy" vanishes. Thus enlightened, a warrior is able to smile with Kashyapa. That smile can strike terror in the heart of one who confronts him or her in battle. Yet it can also be a radiant sign, if properly interpreted, even a seed of peace planted in the midst of conflict.

Of course, a warrior may mistakenly construe another person—or death itself—as "the enemy." But just as Krishna had revealed to Arjuna in the Bhagavad Gita, for the Zen warrior, too, desire is the only enemy. From desire springs both fear and hatred, the true sources of any conflict. The principal strategy for defeating this enemy is persistence in zazen, sitting meditation, the basic exercise of Zen Buddhism. The goal of zazen is not the cultivation of some experience or condition separate from the discipline itself. The purpose of zazen is zazen; that is, to transform the self in such a way that this manner of sitting, breathing, and paying attention is rendered thoroughly dispositional. The danger that such habit-formation will have spiritually stultifying effects can be avoided only insofar as the practice is one that re-

mains "self-watchful," with all habits being checked and governed by mushin as a kind of meta-habit.

The samurai warrior's code *(bushidō)* included loyalty among
its various components. Nevertheless, one could argue that this
virtue is the spiritual core of bushidō, rather than merely a part
of the larger whole. (Once again, such an argument is fueled by
an assessment of the logic governing certain prescriptive utterances in the literature under survey; it is not a historical claim
about the actual conduct and character of specific Japanese
warriors). Nitobe traced the roots of an emphasis on loyalty
in Japanese chivalry back to Shintō and Confucian ideologies
defining the relationship between samurai warriors and their
sovereigns, and not specifically to Zen Buddhism.[32] Yet it is possible to discern a crucial Zen influence here as well. Indeed, some
understanding of mushin, as well as of the Zen perspective on
death and dying, is presupposed by any thorough treatment of
the concept of loyalty in bushidō. To bind oneself in loyalty to
another person is a supreme act of indifference, a powerful exercise in detachment, the putting to death of ego and self-interest.

Loyalty is the greatest virtue prescribed for the warrior; the
perfect embodiment of that virtue represents his highest goal.
Nothing is better for the samurai than to die in the service of his
lord, not even success in defeating the enemy. (Of course, from
the enlightened Zen perspective already sketched here, that dying, if it is simultaneously a dying to self-as-ego, is the only real
victory worth achieving.) Loyalty can demand the voluntary embracing of poverty and can require extraordinary endurance in
the fulfillment of duty. It is a form of devotion to another that
manifests itself in heroic service. Yet it should always be a devotion freely given, presupposing a high level of self-control and
never involving the sacrifice of conscience to the "capricious
will" of one's lord.[33] Such freedom is essential since loyalty can
become problematic in certain cases. One ought not to be loyal
to ignoble persons or causes (for the samurai whose conscience

severely conflicted with the will of a sovereign, ritual suicide, rather than disobedience, was considered the more appropriate course of action).

The relationship defined by the virtue of loyalty is, then, one of neither enslavement nor natural affection. Precisely because his performance of duty is voluntary and self-controlled, the loyal samurai is no slave. At the same time, willingness to die in loyal service to another is different from the sort of motivation that can result in self-sacrifice for a loved one. The quality of service rendered and the strength of the bond of loyalty does not wax and wane with changes in how one feels. It is a matter of morality, as well as of political or civic responsibility. That is not to deny that there can be a mingling of duty with affection in the service required by filial piety or friendship, in the actions of parents toward children, or in the mutual responsibilities of spouses. To admit that this is so is just to suggest that those relationships, too, can demand a measure of loyalty. At the same time, the code of bushidō represents a purer case. There the virtue is cast in stark relief, the abandonment of self-interest that it presupposes being fully exposed and its ethical dimension clearly delineated.

Talk about loyalty might seem at first to fit less naturally and comfortably into a discussion of meditation and the martial arts than, for example, talk about mushin or about the cultivation and circulation of qi within the body. Yet it is important to observe that all the spiritual disciplines explored here could, as strategies of self-cultivation, readily become exercises in self-absorption if their moral and social purposes were to be ignored. From the Buddhist perspective, human beings are always already beings-in-relation. Zazen may appear to be a solitary exercise, but the empty space that it creates within the self is vast enough to contain a world. Zazen is not preparation for anything beside itself, but the ideal is that all of life's practices should be transformed into zazen, so that it does eventually come to represent a way of being with others.

The conflicts in which samurai warriors engaged—bloody manifestations of greed and hatred perhaps far more often than living embodiments of the ideal portrayed here—long ago faded into history. However, the Zen-inspired code of bushidō, like the martial ideology of the Bhagavad Gita, embodies a wisdom that is not limited in significance to the historical period of its formulation. Who or what is sovereign for the contemporary Zen practitioner? To whom does such a person owe loyalty? Where does his or her duty lie? These questions have no simple or immediate answers, but to ignore them altogether may be to risk the serious impoverishment of spiritual exercise.

The concept of jihad is so essential to the self-understanding of Muslims that it is often referred to as the "sixth pillar" of Islam. Among non-Muslims, on the other hand, it is a concept that is notorious for being quite frequently misunderstood. Even within Islam, it is a term with a broad range of applications. *Jihad* is the noun form of the verb *jāhada*, meaning literally to struggle, or to exert oneself.[34] Although the word is often translated, misleadingly, as "holy war," it more accurately refers to a vigorous striving to do the will of God. Of course, such striving can take the form of violent combat with the enemies of Allah. Many of the teachings about jihad in the Quran concern the propriety of this sort of fighting, the conditions under which it becomes a religious duty for Muslims, and the heavenly rewards attached to dying a martyr's death while engaged in such a conflict.

Striving in the way of God does not always consist in violent acts of warfare. The struggle to bring other persons to the truth of Islam can be pursued by peaceful means, as when the Quran instructs Muslims: "Call men to the path of your Lord with wisdom and kindly exhortation. Reason with them in the most courteous manner. Your Lord best knows those who stray from His path and those who are rightly guided."[35] Here, the task of religious education is itself conceived as a form of jihad, a jihad of the tongue or the pen, rather than the sword.

Even more basic is the meaning of jihad as moral exertion or spiritual struggle. This is the usual sense of the word as it is encountered within the literature of Islamic spirituality. Generally, Muslims distinguish between the "lesser" and the "greater jihad." The former designates armed warfare between Muslims and their enemies, the latter, the type of spiritual combat now under consideration—a struggle internal to the soul. The origin of the distinction is one of the traditional utterances of Muhammad *(hadīth)*. Upon returning to Medina after having won a victory in a minor battle, the Prophet announced: "We have now returned from the Smaller Jihad to the Greater Jihad." Queried about the meaning of the "greater jihad," Muhammad responded that it was "the jihad against oneself."[36]

Who, more precisely, is the enemy in this struggle? In the traditional theology of Islam, the self is a complex combination of faculties and impulses. The spiritual life involves the continual conflict between the core, or "heart" *(qalb)*, of the self and a person's lower nature *(nafs)*. It is the latter against which one wages the greater jihad. *Nafs* is to be understood as "the principle of man's spontaneous self-assertion, the seat of his egoistic tendencies and evil inclinations, the carnal force of his concupiscent drives, and the source of his 'a-theistic' self-centeredness."[37] The nafs is not simply a corrupt and corrupting aspect of the self; it is the locus of satanic forces within the self, their base of operations, so that the war waged on the interior battleground of the soul is combat with an evil that infects but also transcends the human individual.

Purification with water is the standard preparation for prayer in the Islamic tradition, somewhat comparable to misogi in the Japanese context. Yet Rumi, the great thirteenth-century Sufi mystic and poet, described the cleansing with water as a precondition only for the "form" of prayer. The necessary precondition for the proper "spirit" of prayer is the extended campaign against evil that constitutes the greater jihad. "The prophets and saints do not avoid spiritual combat. The first spiritual combat they undertake in their quest is the killing of the ego and the abandonment of personal wishes and sensual desires. This is the Greater Holy War."[38] The stakes here are extraordinarily high, since the Quran teaches that only those persons who have "curbed their souls' desires shall dwell in Paradise."[39] Interestingly, the goal in this conflict is not to destroy but to control the nafs. Everything, including one's lower nature, must be made to serve God; even Satan must be made to submit to the divine will.[40] The initial objective of the greater jihad is to achieve self-mastery; the ultimate aim is to surrender the entire self to Allah in perfect and loving submission.

Numerous weapons can be employed in this conflict. Among them are acts of asceticism (such as fasting or abstention from sleep in the form of nightly vigils), the study and recitation of scripture, and conformity to the law of Islam. Ascetic discipline provides a means for acting directly in opposition to the temptations and impulses of the self's lower nature; study and obedience are methods for bringing order to the soul, creating habits of behavior in which the nafs is subdued and then carefully regulated.

Perhaps the most potent weapon in the arsenal of the pious Muslim, however, is the "sword of concentration"—the careful exercise of attention in meditative prayer. When wielded in spiritual combat, this weapon can take a variety of forms, but in every case its purpose is the same: to foster the constant "recollection" (dhikr), or awareness, of God's presence.[41] When the mind is trained in loving attention on God, the devotee is able to meet any challenge successfully, whether it arises from within or from without. The Quran teaches that "in the remembrance of Allah all hearts are comforted."[42] In its simplest form, the practice of dhikr is the continuous remembrance of God through the repetitive invocation of the divine name. Such prayer can be practiced under any circumstances and is not restricted to the special times set aside during each day for ritual prayer. It can be uttered loudly, softly, or made in silence. Here prayer is reduced to its essence as a simple act of attention.

The invocation of God's name should never become a meaningless ritual. To be mindful of God's ubiquitous presence requires also that one should be unceasingly thankful for it. As in Ueshiba's philosophy, the cultivation of religious awareness is simultaneously the fostering of a sense of gratitude. "Remember Me, then, and I will remember you. Give thanks to Me and never deny Me."[43] The Quran explicitly links dhikr to *shukr,* prayerful acts of recollection to the heartfelt expression of gratitude. Everything that exists is a gift and, hence, the sign of a divine giver. Among the Sufis, even feelings of gratitude are the kind of thing for which one ought to be thankful. Creatures exist in a relationship of radical dependence on God; to remember Allah is also to attend to that relationship and to recognize the profoundly gratuitous quality of all creation.

Among the features linking the internal martial arts both to yoga and to the Buddhist practice of zazen are the emphases on the regulation of the breath and on the disposition of the body (regarding either posture or movement). The attention to these physical phenomena is by no means absent in Muslim spirituality. Dhikr, for example, a practice characterized by the element of redundancy, the repeated invocation of the name of God as a mantra, is often done audibly and in the form of chanting (it can also involve the use of rosary beads for the systematic counting of the various divine names). Thus, dhikr supplies a rhythm that can then be utilized to measure or modify the pattern of breathing. In this sense, it is a very basic form of breathing meditation (although it can also assume much more complex forms, following precise formulas for the coordination of breath with utterance and intention).[44]

Interestingly, the Arabic term *nafs* is somewhat ambiguous in meaning. Although it typically denotes the baser aspect of the self, it can also designate "the vital principle of life-breath" in human beings, the cessation of which results in death.[45] This ambiguity suggests a possible connection between the strategy of regulating the breath and the general strategy within the greater jihad of subduing evil impulses. Recall that the explicit purpose of jihad is not the complete destruction of the lower nature, but rather success in the struggle to control it. Dhikr achieves just such a purpose, harmonizing mind, heart, voice, and breath in the continuous act of remembering/naming/ thanking Allah.

From an Islamic perspective, the body is a battleground. Moreover, breathing is a process to which the Muslim devotee (especially in esoteric Islam) must carefully attend in the practice of meditation. What, then, is the potential religious significance of physical posture and movement? There is nothing in Islam comparable to the extraordinarily detailed cultivation of āsana in Hindu yoga. The tradition does prescribe appropriate postures for kneeling, sitting, or standing in prayer and meditation, but these prescriptions do not appear to have any kind of elaborate theological rationale. There is also a tradition of internal alchemy within Sufi mysticism, similar to the employment of alchemical imagery by Daoists and Hindus in their mapping of complex processes of spiritual transformation.

More intriguing is a comparison of the constantly spiraling, circular movements in aikidō and baguazhang with the rapid, whirling, rhythmic movements of the dervishes in Sufi Islam. It has even been suggested that the latter practice, in its earliest form, may have been patterned on the ritual dances of Arab warriors, so that there could be an actual historical connection with some ancient form of martial art.[46] Even in the absence of such a connection, the martial significance of the dervish's movements is clear: this is a form of dancing dhikr, the blending of mind, sound, breath, and body in the ecstatic overcoming of the ego. Rumi captures something of the martial flavor of the dance in his verses: "Dance where you can break your own self and pluck out the cotton from the wound of sensuality! People dance and frolic in the square—men dance in their own blood. When they have been delivered from their own hands, they clap their hands; when they have jumped outside of their own im-perfection, they dance. . . . Dance everything other than Him under your feet!"[47]

The dervish utilizes music and movement in order to en-hance devotion, to focus a loving attention on God. Just as plan-ets orbit the sun, the dancer traces ecstatic circles around the di-vine center of devotion. But the rapidly spinning motions of the dance are also a method for silencing the noisy, self-assertive ego, a strategy already encountered in the internal martial disci-plines. The focusing of attention is simultaneously an exercise in self-emptying. It *is* a warrior's dance, the dance of jihad; from an ideal perspective, it is also a victory dance. Ironically, the spoils of victory, the riches of war in a war thus waged and won, fre-quently will be described by the Muslim mystic as the achieve-ment of poverty *(faqr)*.

The embracing of an outward poverty is a spiritual discipline in which the Sufi is prone to engage as a rudimentary exercise. The deeper meaning of faqr, however, is captured in the concept of spiritual poverty, the lack of any desire for wealth and worldly goods,[48] which extends even to the afterlife: it is detachment from need for any kind of personal pleasure or reward. This atti-tude combines with gratitude and patience *(sabr)* in the rich Muslim portrayal of spiritual perfection—spiritual victory. The person who embodies such perfection has achieved a precious equanimity (compare the ideal of "sameness-and-indifference" in the yoga philosophy), a calm readiness for whatever God chooses to give, whether it be blessing or affliction. In contrast, the person still controlled by nafs is dramatically affected by any changes in circumstance, by every stroke of fortune or misfor-tune, victimized by forces both internal and external. The chief fruit of victory in the spiritual combat is a poverty that manifests itself as freedom.

The consequence of victory may be freedom, but the goal of jihad is the overcoming of anyone or anything that violates the divine will. The essence of Islam is submission to Allah, a surrender that results, paradoxically, in victory, in the self's liberation. Everything that exists must be brought into such a state of submission. The above discussion has been concentrated almost entirely on the "greater jihad," the holy war waged by each person on the interior battleground of the soul. There exists a massive religious and legal literature in Islam, none of it examined here, concerning the principles that ought to govern the struggle as it occurs *among* human beings rather than *within* them—the "lesser jihad." Yet even this brief analysis should have demonstrated that the two types of conflict cannot be neatly or perfectly separated from one another. Victory in the internal struggle will dramatically determine how an individual responds to other persons or interprets external situations. The weapons that brought success on one front—loving attention to God, constant gratitude, poverty of spirit—are not suddenly to be discarded in this broader conflict.

According to the teachings of Islam, one of the chief obstacles in the struggle against one's own lower impulses is confusion about how the battle is actually going. A sense that victory is close at hand can sometimes be the work of Satan, who cooperates with the human ego to create in persons a false sense of confidence, a dangerous spiritual pride. (This analysis of the internal conflict closely resembles the one sketched by Saint Ignatius in his theology of the spiritual life, examined in the next chapter.) As a result, one of the chief weapons required by any warrior is interpretive skill, a power of discernment to be exercised in precisely those situations where one is uncertain about how the battle is going or exactly where the real enemy lies. Such discernment would seem essential for every form of jihad. But failure to employ it successfully on the interior battleground could clearly have disastrous consequences in the wider, public realm. If one cannot recognize the devious persistence of one's own ego as enemy, how can one hope to judge one's true enemies under any circumstance?

It might be worth noting, in concluding these remarks, that Rumi identified the most vigorous type of jihad as occurring in the encounter not with enemies but with friends or "companions." To the extent that they are pious or of a saintly disposition, such persons represent for the devotee a most serious challenge; they wield a terrible power. "Acts of spiritual combat are of many kinds, the greatest of which is mixing with companions who have turned their faces toward God and their backs toward the world. No act of spiritual combat is more difficult than to sit with sound companions, for the very sight of them wastes away the ego and annihilates it."[49] This idea of "sitting with companions," exposing oneself and one's ego to the spiritual power of saintly example, is a remarkable suggestion of how the waging of a holy war (not just as an internal but as a kind of interpersonal struggle) might be conceived from the perspective of Muslim martial spirituality.

FOUR

The Spiritual Combat

The Gospel narratives in the Christian New Testament confront their reader with the challenge of reconciling two different teachings that appear to stand in tension with one another. Each of them is challenging in itself, placing radical demands on the Christian disciple. Consider, first, this warning given by Jesus: "Do not think that I have come to bring peace to the earth; I have not come to bring peace, but a sword. For I have come to set a man against his father, and a daughter against her mother, and a daughter-in-law against her mother-in-law; and one's foes will be members of one's own household."[1] Elsewhere, in what seems to represent a sharp contrast in perspective, he restrained one of his followers who was fighting to resist Jesus' arrest in Gethsemane, telling him: "Put your sword back into its place; for all who take the sword will perish by the sword."[2] Earlier, Jesus had instructed his disciples to adopt a strategy even more radical than restraint from violence: "Love your enemies, do good to those who hate you, bless those who curse you, pray for those who abuse you. If anyone strikes you on the cheek, offer the other also; and from anyone who takes away your coat do not withhold even your shirt."[3]

The first teaching affirmed that the Christian was inevitably engaged in some kind of conflict, much as Paul later indicated in his letter to the Ephesians when he sought to prepare them for combat by reviewing the martial resources at their disposal. The fact that these resources were spiritual in character should not distract the reader from the seriousness with which Paul perceived the enemy as a threat. The second type of instruction quickly undermined any simplistic understanding of the nature of that threat and the response that it required. Who exactly was the enemy here? How was that enemy to be resisted and overcome?

The idea of a "spiritual combat" is deeply embedded in the Christian theological tradition, as these scriptural sources clearly illustrate; but that idea is certainly much older than Christianity itself. In antiquity, the belief that the world is a battleground between spiritual forces of good and evil is most dramatically embodied in the ideology and mythology of Zoroastrianism, a religion that originated in ancient Iran (late in the second millennium before the common era). Based on the teachings of the prophet Zoroaster, its theology is organized around belief in Ahura Mazda, God, who is conceived as being uncreated and eternal, perfectly wise and benevolent. This deity, the creator of the world, is opposed by Angra Mainyu, an evil and destructive spirit. All free creatures must choose between Truth and the Lie. The evil one and those beings allied with him have opted to oppose the Truth. Zoroaster summoned his followers actively to resist this evil, to exercise their freedom in embracing the Truth by performing righteous deeds. The power of God cannot be compromised by evil; the eventual destruction of all that is evil, in a terrible judgment of fire, is guaranteed. Until that moment of final judgment, however, the world remains an arena of conflict, as does the spirit of every free creature confronted with the choice between good and evil.[4]

The relevance of this synopsis of ancient Persian beliefs to a Christian theology of the spiritual combat is exposed by the insight that Zoroastrianism exerted considerable influence over the development of certain ideas within Judaism and, through Judaism, impacted Christianity as well.[5] Released from the oppressive Babylonian hegemony, Israel was first exposed to Zoroaster's theology when it fell under the benevolent sovereignty of the conquering Cyrus of Persia (sixth century B.C.E.). At a later period, these Zoroastrian ideas blended with other elements characteristic of Hellenistic Judaism, providing a fertile soil for the germination of Gnosticism. Historically, much early Christian talk about spiritual warfare appears to have been shaped by Gnostic ideas, revealing, however indirectly, Christianity's ancient Iranian legacy.

In the postbiblical period, the spiritual combat continued to rage, nowhere more violently than in the deserts of Egypt and Syria, whence Christian monks withdrew to confront the enemy directly. Hermits like Saint Antony struggled to achieve in their daily spiritual practice the ideal succinctly articulated in *1 Thessalonians:* "Rejoice always, pray without ceasing, give thanks in all circumstances; for this is the will of God in Christ Jesus for you."[6] In the silent heat of the desert, these monks were challenged by the "demon of noontide," an oppressive boredom *(acedia)* carrying with it the potential for every kind of distraction. Never entirely safe from a foe bent on disrupting their prayerful meditations, an enemy fully determined, by whatever means possible, to "capture" their attention, they were most vulnerable at midday, with the onset of fatigue, the sun at its hottest, and the spiritual labors of afternoon and evening still stretched out before them.[7]

The Christian monk's battle with himself—with his temptations, desires, distractions—was always first to be understood within the much broader context of a campaign against the devil and his allies. In his hagiography of Antony, Athanasius described the saint's frequently violent encounters with demonic forces, spirits that assumed every manner of beastly form, invading his cell and threatening to overwhelm him. Throughout Antony's ordeal, "the state of his soul was one of purity, for it was not constricted by grief, nor relaxed by pleasure, nor affected by either laughter or dejection. . . . He maintained utter equilibrium, like one guided by reason and steadfast in that which accords with nature."[8] In his discourses, Antony exhorted his fellow monks to cultivate the same sort of equanimity while maintaining a constant vigilance in prayer:

Let the contest be ours, so that anger does not rule us or desire over-whelm us, for it is written: *The anger of man does not work the right-eousness of God,* and *desire, when it has conceived, gives birth to sin; and sin, when it is full grown, brings forth death.* Conducting our lives in this manner, let us carefully keep watch, and as Scripture says, let us *keep* our *heart in all watchfulness.* For we have terrible and villainous ene-mies—the evil demons, and our *contending* is against these, as the Apostle said—*not against flesh and blood, but against the principalities, against the powers, against the world rulers of this present darkness, against the spiritual hosts of wickedness in the heavenly places.*[9]

While Athanasius's biography vividly portrayed Antony as an extraordinary spiritual athlete capable of the most rigorous sort of asceticism, his account was also at pains to show that no level of proficiency in spiritual exercises can insure an individual's vic-tory over evil. It is the surrender to Christ and complete trust in the divine power and mercy that provide such a guarantee. The work of spiritual exercise is always already something being worked in and through the saint by divine grace *(theopoiesis);* it is less adequately conceived as an act of self-transformation than as a willingness that the self should be transformed, a gradual overcoming of any resistance to the effects of grace. In one par-ticularly graphic illustration of the need for total reliance on God in the spiritual combat, Antony was surrounded by demons in a "tomb" into which he had retreated to pray; severely beaten and wounded, but steadfast in purpose, he was rescued when the roof suddenly opened and a beam of light descended, causing the demons to vanish.[10]

In the history of early Christianity, it was both the call to mar-tyrdom and the summons to embrace asceticism (the latter sup-plementing but then gradually supplanting the former) that stimulated theological reflection concerning the spiritual com-bat.[11] Martyrdom and asceticism each necessitated the cultiva-tion of martial virtues, especially courage in the face of powers hostile to the faith. The martyr might have to endure death at the hands of these enemies, but, like Antony, every saintly ascetic knew that sin also "brings forth death," so the threat of destruction, even if reconfigured, was never ignored. In the medieval period, this vagueness persisted. The threat of death could be physical or spiritual (only the latter ought to be feared by the Christian). The battleground for the spiritual combat could be external or internal. The enemy could manifest itself in a great variety of ways.

In his *Summa Theologica*, Thomas Aquinas identified the sacrament of confirmation as a gift of God specifically intended to prepare the Christian for the rigors of spiritual warfare. "In this sacrament the Holy Ghost is given for strength in spiritual combat." The tracing with chrism of a cross on the forehead of the recipient "is the sign which is given to the combatant, as in bodily combat: thus are soldiers marked with the signs of their leaders. And to this refer the words, *I sign thee with the sign of the cross*, in which sign, to wit, our king triumphed."[12] It is important to review one of the distinctions that Aquinas made between this sacrament and baptism. The symbolism of baptism primarily "refers to the man to be sanctified." In contrast, confirmation "is ordained not only to the sanctification of man in himself, but also to strengthen him in his outward combat. Consequently, not only is mention made of interior sanctification, in the words, *I confirm thee with the chrism of salvation:* but furthermore, man is signed outwardly, as it were with the standard of the cross, unto the outward spiritual combat; and this is signified by the words, *I sign thee with the sign of the cross.*"[13]

Note that the combat for which this sacrament prepares its recipient is described here as being "spiritual" yet "outward." Again, a certain vagueness persists; this combat could take numerous forms. But its being "spiritual" does not necessarily reduce it to the status of some private, interior conflict; rather, even if the enemy strikes at (or from) the innermost depths of a person's soul, the ensuing conflict has a definite public status, which is why in the sacrament a "man is signed outwardly." Moreover, it is not a battle that the individual wages alone. Not only do these Christian soldiers bear the mark of their "leader," the standard of the cross, but the strength with which they fight is the strength of the Holy Spirit, a supernatural power by which they have been inwardly transformed.

Aquinas's extended consideration of the virtue of fortitude is also relevant to the present discussion.[14] Fortitude was a gift of the Holy Spirit for Aquinas, a firmness of mind that is required to accomplish anything good as well as to resist anything evil. It is manifested as the courage with which a soldier or a martyr is able to overcome the fear of death and to endure tremendous suffering. Yet this virtue is not restricted in meaning to its application in such instances. Aquinas conceived of patience, for example, as a special aspect of the virtue of fortitude. Following Augustine, he understood patience to be a kind of equanimity, a special disposition to bear evil "with an equal mind, without being disturbed by sorrow." Such a virtue is essential for the practice of meditation, a patience born of love *(caritas)* that enables the devotee to withstand and eventually overcome the threat of acedia and all its progeny.

Although the discussion cannot be pursued here beyond the level of a suggestion, the potential significance of the thought of Duns Scotus for understanding the theology of the spiritual combat ought to observed.[15] Scotus was a medieval Franciscan writing in the period immediately after Aquinas, complementing but also sometimes criticizing Thomistic perspectives. It is Scotus's voluntarism, his emphasis on the primacy and the efficacy of the will, that deserves special attention here. While he infrequently employed a martial vocabulary, Scotus nevertheless distinguished two inclinations in the will; an affection for advantage and the affection for justice. The former is an essentially egoistic impulse *(affectio commodi)* that, if not checked by the inclination to affirm the value of things in themselves *(affectio justitiae)* can result in monstrous evil. Freedom of the will exists for Scotus because the self is not determined by a single inclination; in this respect, freedom consists in a certain indeterminacy. Because of the presence of an affection for justice, the self is able to exercise freedom, to achieve self-transcendence, rather than being entirely constrained by its nature and the ego's natural desires.

This analysis of the will's two inclinations, which often are in conflict with one another, is consistent with a Christian understanding (evident already in Paul's letters) of the self as an arena of spiritual combat. Much as the Muslim theologians had emphasized in their portrayal of the greater jihad, for Scotus the ideal in the exercise of freedom was the control of the egoistic inclination, not its elimination or destruction. Spiritual and moral discipline are aimed at self-control, the harmonizing and appropriate ordering of inclinations. Moreover, the self displays its power of freedom, the efficacy of volition, not only in the choices that it makes but also in its steadfast commitment *(firmitas)* to ends already chosen. This quality of steadfastness, resonant both with Aquinas's treatment of fortitude and with the emphasis on loyalty in the samurai warrior's code, can also be conceived as a martial virtue.

Like Morihei Ueshiba, but centuries earlier, the young Ignatius of Loyola was carefully trained in the various arts of war, and his early manhood was similarly marked by the traumatic experiences of a soldier in combat. The cannonball that destroyed his leg in battle also helped to precipitate the spiritual crisis that led to his conversion. The wounded soldier moved from one kind of battlefield to another.

Embodied in Ignatius's decision to pursue the religious life was his discovery of an "equivalent discipline" for war:[16] "It is my will to conquer the whole world and all my enemies, and thus to enter into the glory of my Father. Therefore, whoever wishes to join me in this must be willing to labor with me, that by following me in suffering, he may follow me in glory."[17] In his meditation on the "The Kingdom of Christ," proposed for the end of the first week of the spiritual exercises, Ignatius asked devotees to imagine Christ delivering such a summons. The martial imagery that characterizes the discourse is commonplace at this point in Ignatius's text (a manual that sketches roughly four weeks of meditations, with some additional instructions attached). Even in his "Introductory Observations," Ignatius included a considerable body of practical advice for thwarting the "enemy," the evil one who works constantly to undermine the practice of meditation. For example, he encouraged each exercitant, during those times when he is most besieged by distractions and temptations, to continue in prayer for "a little more than the full hour" set aside for that purpose. "Thus he will accustom himself not only to resist the enemy, but even to overthrow him."[18]

Additional strategies of the same sort were appended to the end of the text in the "Rules for the Discernment of Spirits." A careful reading of these rules reveals the extent to which Ignatius's martial spirituality was thoroughly semiotic in character. As in the martial arts, also in Islamic jihad, so, too, for Ignatius: to be successful in battle is to be skilled in the art of interpretation, in distinguishing enemies from friends, and in unraveling the logic that governs an enemy's strategy. All signs are potentially multivalent. Ignatius's rules do not assign determinate meanings to specific signs as they appear. Patience, detachment, and self-criticism are the crucial elements required for skill in interpretation. But what, more precisely, are the signs to which Ignatius directed his readers' attention? Anything, conceivably, can serve as a sign of God's will and purposes. Consequently, virtually anything can be a counterfeit sign masking the devil's wicked purposes. In the "Rules," however, Ignatius limited his discussion to the significance of certain describable moods or feelings.

The enemy that preoccupied Ignatius typically wages war on a landscape interior to the self, frequently causing an individual to endure intense feelings of "desolation." Ignatius understood desolation as a "darkness of soul, turmoil of spirit, inclination to what is low and earthly, restlessness arising from many disturbances and temptations which lead to want of faith, want of hope, want of love. The soul is wholly slothful, tepid, sad, and separated, as it were, from its Creator and Lord."[19] This is the same enemy, employing the same strategy, that Saint Antony had encountered in the emptiness and heat of the Egyptian desert.

In Ignatius's view, such feelings of desolation were to be endured with the kind of courage and perseverance that would be demanded of a soldier in the midst of a violent battle. The soldier's failure could result in injury or death, for himself or his comrades. The consequences of a failure of nerve on the part of the religious devotee are potentially even more dangerous, a spiritual death, the loss of eternal life. "If one begins to be afraid and lose courage in temptations," Ignatius warned, "no wild animal on earth can be more fierce than the enemy of our human nature. He will carry out his perverse intentions with consummate malice."[20]

So malicious is the enemy that it can attack the human psyche even with feelings of consolation or joyfulness, creating in it a sense of complacency and false pride, causing a corresponding weakness of will. Moreover, feelings of desolation may not be the work of the devil at all; they could be the result of God's "trying" or testing the individual—a military exercise, so to speak, rather than an actual encounter with the evil one.[21] In either case, such assaults are to be patiently endured, but the key to distinguishing between cases is the cultivation of a certain power of discernment. Patience itself, the ability to "wait," is not irrelevant to the task of discernment. But it presupposes also a profound spirit of indifference, the "first principle and foundation" of the spiritual exercises. This *indiferencia* (exercised primarily as a resistance to the hegemony of one's personal preferences and inclinations) is manifested as a readiness to meet the enemy anywhere, also a constant readiness to discern and then submit to the will of God. Being "without any inordinate attachment," such a person is "like a balance at equilibrium," inclined in no particular direction and so prepared to follow the path that God chooses, wherever it may lead.[22]

From this Ignatian perspective, the feelings of desolation to which God may subject the individual can serve multiple purposes. This trial could be a straightforward test of patience or a more complex exercise intended to undermine habitual expectations, and thus, to foster a sense of detachment. It is interesting that Ignatius compared the appropriately indifferent person to a balance at "equilibrium," this being the same word that Athanasius used in his *Life* to depict the state of Antony's soul. Consider, also, the basic similarity between this image and the ideal of "sameness-and-indifference" that Krishna preached to Arjuna. (Ironically, this is also the sort of spiritual condition that one aspires to cultivate in the practice of taijiquan by *avoiding* "double-weightedness." When the goal of the practice is constant movement, the image of what constitutes an ideal equilibrium is itself dramatically transformed.)

Meditations like the one on "The Kingdom of Christ" in the first week and on the "Two Standards" in the second week of the exercises explicitly invoke the idea of war and lean heavily on the use of martial imagery. Clearly Ignatius's purpose was to arouse in devotees the sort of powerful emotions that are typically linked to the phenomena that he portrayed. This seems especially true of the meditation on the "Two Standards," where the exercitant is instructed to form a mental representation of the army of Christ arrayed on a vast plain near Jerusalem beneath the banner of their "Commander-in-Chief."[23] Opposed to this array is the equally massive army of Satan, mobilized on a plain near Babylon, their chief "seated on a great throne of fire and smoke." The images presented here are of real armies of soldiers organized in identifiable geographical locations. But the strategy delineated for each army makes clear the nature of the combat in which they are about to engage. Satan's hordes will first use riches, then honor, then pride to attack the followers of Christ. "From these three steps, the evil one leads to all other vices." In response, Christians must embrace poverty, a desire for contempt, and humility. "From these three steps, let them lead men to all other virtues."

Poverty is the first weapon that Ignatius identified as essential for the counterattack on Satan's hordes. As in Sufi spirituality, this concept could signify a literal poverty of riches or a deeper poverty of spirit. The embrace of actual poverty, like the desire for contempt, does not violate Ignatius's first principle of indifference, insofar as it represents a sincere wish to imitate Christ and to share in his suffering. But God's will always trumps human wishes; that is, a person may in fact receive honor and riches instead of being denied them. In either case, the Christian should be indifferent to them—again, like a balance at equilibrium.

Poverty and humility are powerful spiritual dispositions, obviously crucial for success in the battle against the forces of darkness. Ignatius's terse instructions were not limited, however, to the task of identifying lofty spiritual ideals. The text of the *Spiritual Exercises* is also marked by its pragmatism, its attention to practical details and to specific strategies that might facilitate the practice of meditation. This sort of pragmatism is clearly evident in the "Rules for the Discernment of Spirits," briefly discussed above. It is also a distinctive feature of Ignatius's "Three Methods of Prayer."[24]

The first of the three methods, as Ignatius himself admitted, is not so much a method of prayer as it is a designation of subject matter suitable for meditation. Among the items identified here as worthy of attention are the ten commandments and the seven capital sins, with special consideration being devoted to the manner in which the exercitant has successfully avoided the latter while adhering to the former. The "Three Methods" appear toward the end of Ignatius's text. Yet it is important to observe how frequently throughout the exercises, but especially in the first week, the type of Christian meditation that he prescribed took the form of an "examination of conscience." The enemy's goal is to inflate the ego and turn it away in its arrogance from loyal obedience to Christ. The Christian soldier's first sally in countering the devil must be a humble examination of fault—of actual sin and of all the dispositional sources of sin.

Additional topics considered suitable for meditation are the "three powers of the soul" (memory, understanding, will) and the "five senses of the body." Ignatian meditation is distinguished from much classical Buddhist and Hindu meditation (though perhaps not from all forms of Daoist meditation) by the degree to which one is encouraged in its practice imaginatively to engage or "apply" the senses, rather than to withdraw the mind from objects of sense. In this respect, the Ignatian method differs remarkably even from the Carmelite strategy of John of the Cross, another Spanish Catholic saint roughly contemporaneous with Ignatius. The methods may differ, but the goals of practice are essentially the same. Ignatius refused to surrender the senses or the imagination to his adversary, while fully recognizing the manner in which they can be cleverly employed to lead a person into sin. His strategy, through the prayerful exercise of the imagination, was to direct the senses in a way that would foster devotion; as with these other meditative disciplines, Ignatius's ultimate objective was self-control.

The second method of prayer is more accurately labeled, specifying a procedure rather than a particular subject matter for meditation. The method involves taking a standard vocal prayer and beginning to recite it one word at a time. The key element in Ignatius's instruction is that one should "continue meditating" on a single word of prayer without moving on to the next for as long as one "finds various meanings, comparisons, relish, and consolation in the consideration of it." Here Ignatius portrayed a meditative practice that involves a kind of disciplined free association, a somewhat playful mode of thought similar to what the American philosopher Charles Peirce was later to call "musement."

It is easy to see how this method of prayer honors the first principle that Ignatius established as the foundation of the exercises. The regular manner of reciting a frequently recited vocal prayer can quickly become encrusted in habit. Specific images and meanings become fixed in their association with the words of that prayer. This method is intended to loosen those bonds of association or, at the very least, to enrich and expand them. Once again, it is an exercise in detachment, the playful (but always for Ignatius very serious) cultivation of a habit of indifference, permitting the exercitant to discern meanings hitherto suppressed, to perceive how God "dwells" and "works" not in some isolated domain, but in "all creatures."

In the text of his instructions concerning this second method, Ignatius briefly addressed issues of bodily disposition, stipulating that one should close one's eyes in prayer or fix them in position, but not allow them to roam. Sitting and kneeling are both acceptable postures for meditation, the choice depending on which is more "conducive to devotion" for any given individual. This sort of pragmatism pervades all of Ignatius's remarks concerning posture in the exercises. Elsewhere, not only sitting and kneeling but also standing, lying on the ground either prostrate or face up, and walking back and forth are introduced as possibilities for prayer.[25] One should not remain bound to a particular posture, so that if it becomes uncomfortable or otherwise ineffective then one ought to change it, even in the midst of prayer. Here Ignatius displayed a clear recognition of the potential relationship between physical and spiritual dispositions, although his concern was focused on eliminating the body as a distraction, rather than on employing it for positive purposes in meditative practice.

The breath, however, is to be positively utilized; in fact, Ignatius's third method of prayer constitutes a species of breathing meditation. Here the cadence of vocal prayer is regulated by respiration so that with each breath a single word of the prayer is to be recited. Most importantly, for this brief "space of time," the attention is to be directed to that particular word, focused both on its meaning and on the person (most typically God) to whom it is addressed. This Ignatian "yoga" is primitive in comparison with what one encounters in Patañjali, Zen Buddhism, Daoism, or Sufi mysticism. Nevertheless, it is significant that one of the three basic methods of meditation that Ignatius outlined in his manual was a strategy of using the breath to regulate attention.

Ignatius's soldier was a member of a powerful army, not a solitary figure or mercenary. To be sure, the battle that Ignatius described was one fought over individual souls, the fall into vice representing defeat and the cultivation of virtue being an important victory. Nevertheless, the virtuous life was to be lived "for the greater glory of God." Such a life was meaningless as a private phenomenon; it necessarily had a public, communal dimension. Prayer and meditation were the work of preparation for the apostolate. The interior battle with Satan was to be waged as part of a military campaign that involved leading others to Christ; such is the earthly mission of Christ's Church. Moreover, ecclesiastical authority represented for Ignatius a kind of military chain of command. This helps to explain his emphasis in the *Spiritual Exercises* on the virtue of obedience (including its importance as a discipline of detachment), as well as the presence there of a set of "Rules for Thinking with the Church."[26]

Furthermore, the individual devotee is engaged in activity that will succeed only by the grace of God. In that respect, as well, these meditations should never be perceived as a solitary form of engagement. Isolation from Christ and Christ's church would guarantee immediate and overwhelming defeat at the hands of the enemy. Interestingly, in his rules for discernment, Ignatius identified a type of consolation that the Christian can feel certain is a sign of the divine presence, free of the possibility of deception. This occurs when the consolation is "without previous cause," not linked to any particular thought, image, or action that may have preceded and precipitated it. It is a pure, undeserved, and unanticipated gift from God. There could be no clearer indication than this that Ignatius's exercises were never intended as some form of "spiritual technology" for the production of consolation. They are not a simple recipe for achieving some spiritually felicitous condition. They are, rather, an essentially cooperative enterprise, a person's faithful response to grace as gift. The essence of that response is a grateful, loving obedience; for Ignatius, as for Ueshiba, love was the chief weapon in the spiritual soldier's arsenal, a fact evidenced by the culmination of these exercises in his "Contemplation to Obtain the Love of God."

The combat for which Ignatius of Loyola sought to prepare his readers is at least as old as Christianity. In fact, even if one shared all of the narrowly Christian premises that Ignatius affirmed, it would make sense to consider the conflict as older than that; after all, despite the lively history of their relationship with him, Christians certainly did not invent the Devil. Nonetheless, Ignatius was also very much a man of his place and times, a product of the Catholic Reformation in sixteenth-century Europe. His manual for Christian soldiers was to have a decisive impact on the spirituality of that period and beyond. But it was itself shaped by the various struggles within which Roman Catholics then found themselves embroiled. These included not only the "eternal internal" battle with evil, not merely the sorts of military campaigns in which the young Ignatius himself participated, but also the traumatic conflict between the Catholic church and the Protestant reformers perceived as heretics, as well as the struggle by many Catholics to reform the church from within.

Authored somewhat later in the sixteenth century, most probably by Lorenzo Scupoli, an Italian priest of the Theatine order, *The Spiritual Combat* was a product of the same general historical milieu and embodied many of the same intentions as the *Spiritual Exercises*. Those intentions are plainly announced at the beginning of the book, never obscured, and remain clear at its conclusion. Toward the end of the text, Scupoli evaluated what is at stake in the conflict under consideration: "Although our entire life on earth is a continual warfare, it is certain that the last day of battle will be the most dangerous; for he who falls on this day, falls never to rise again."[27] Of course, since one has no precise knowledge of when the "last day of battle" will occur, one would be wise to treat each day as if it were the last. Moreover, each day is significant for what it might contribute to victory in that final encounter with the enemy. "In order, therefore, to be prepared, we must prepare ourselves now; for he who fights well through life will with greater facility emerge victorious in the final assault. Meditate too on death, considering its significance, for such consideration will remove the terror that strikes when death is nigh, and give your mind greater freedom for the combat."

As for the Japanese samurai, fear of death is one of the opponents that must be overcome in the spiritual struggle. But this fear is itself grounded in more basic egoistic impulses, so that in order to eliminate fear it is necessary first to strike at the root of those impulses and at the evil one who feeds them. Although Scupoli fell short of identifying sensuous appetites as evil, they clearly do represent a person's "inferior" nature, that aspect of human nature most vulnerable to the enemy's attack. "The entire spiritual warfare, consequently, consists in this: the rational faculty is placed between the divine will above it and the sensitive appetite below it, and attacked from both sides—God moving it by His grace and the flesh by its appetites strive for victory."[28] Here human reason and volition are caught, at least initially, in a crossfire between the onslaught of divine grace and the "withering attacks" of satanic forces from below. Once again, this war has a cosmic significance that transcends any individual. The individual's fundamental responsibility is to exercise freedom in choosing sides, to become Christ's ally in the spiritual warfare. Once that choice is properly made and persons have become "firmly settled in their way of life," this ambivalence is removed and the sole purpose of life is now victory with and for Christ over evil.

Toward this end, Scupoli identified "four weapons without which it is impossible to gain the victory in this spiritual combat. These four things are: distrust of oneself, confidence in God, proper use of the faculties of body and mind, and the duty of prayer."[29] Most of the sixty-six chapters in the book are devoted to practical discussions of prayer and of the proper use of human faculties. But there is some important early consideration of the other two "weapons." Scupoli's treatment of the first of these, distrust of self, resembles Ignatius's advice concerning the discernment of spirits. In both cases, there is a motivating worry about the relative ease with which even well-intentioned spiritual warriors can fall victim to self-deception. A great deal of the power of evil consists in its devious quality, its taking so frequently the form of a lie (recall Zoroaster's theology). And so vice often masquerades as virtue, evil as something attractive and good, always in order to mislead a person into the false interpretation of an actual or impending defeat as victory (the Greek strategy in conquering the Trojans). Against this tactic, Scupoli warned the Christian to be always on guard. "We must gradually accustom ourselves to distrust our own strength, to dread the illusions of our own mind, the strong tendency of our nature to sin, and the overwhelming number of enemies that surround us. Their subtlety, experience, and strength surpass ours, for they can transform themselves into angels of light and lie in ambush for us as we advance towards heaven."[30]

There can be nothing momentary or occasional about this distrust of self if it is to have any value as a weapon in the battle with evil. It must, instead, become a well-entrenched tendency, a habit of self-criticism, a constant vigilance. Moreover, it is relatively useless by itself. That is to say, one of the insights that facilitates this habitual tendency is the awareness that "we cannot, without divine assistance, accomplish the smallest good or advance the smallest step toward heaven." And so, while absolutely necessary in the spiritual combat, this distrust of self must be joined to complete confidence in God if it is to have any efficacy.

The ego's abandoning of its own limited resources is related dialectically to a complete trust in the infinite power of the Deity.

Scupoli described a test that might serve to indicate the extent to which these two weapons are being effectively employed. When a person "commits a fault," it is important to observe whether or not "he yields to anger and despairs of advancing in the way of virtue."[31] Insofar as this occurs, such a person has not yet abandoned an arrogant self-confidence, has failed to trust entirely in God. One properly disposed will feel a sorrow for the fault committed, but see it as a signal that greater distrust in self and reliance on God are required. Consequently, this sorrow will be "accompanied by peace of mind." It will not undermine the strategy already laid down for the spiritual combat and so, unlike anger and despair, it will not "prevent the pursuit of his enemies to their final destruction."

As Scupoli turned to the lengthy consideration of the felicitous employment of faculties and the importance of prayer, three basic qualities were established as essential for the Christian combatant: detachment, self-control, and equanimity, or peace of mind. Like Ignatius of Loyola, Scupoli was concerned about the oppressive power of "inordinate attachments." He warned that the will is often moved to embrace or reject an object before the understanding has been able carefully to evaluate it. Judgment is thus polluted by passion and the true nature of things is effectively obscured. By contrast, "Happy are those who strip themselves of all attachments to creatures and then endeavor to discover the true nature of things before they permit their affections to be attached."[32] Here again is the semiotic insight that links all of these various forms of martial spirituality: the meaning of a sign is accessible only to one who is appropriately detached, predisposed in advance to embrace no particular meaning and thus ready to interpret whatever is being communicated through the sign.

This detachment is also the key to achieving an important measure of self-control. "We must control our minds and not permit them to wander aimlessly about. Our minds must become insensible to mundane projects, to gossip, to the feverish search for news. Our indifference to the affairs of this world must give them a dream-like quality."[33] This control is important precisely because a wandering mind is one most vulnerable to the enemy's advances. Not just worldly imaginings, but even an undisciplined contemplation of spiritual goods can prove to be a fertile source of distractions. It is easy for such a mind to become "drugged with a false sense of appreciation of God." Inflated pride in the powers of the understanding; unwarranted self-confidence; a growing sense of the need to rely on no one but oneself . . . Scupoli's diagnosis of such a state of mind is explicit: "It is a deadly, almost incurable disease."

This sort of assessment will seem purely hyperbolic unless the existential context supplied by the spiritual combat is presupposed. Scupoli never relinquished such a perspective. "This war is unavoidable," he warned, "and you must either fight or die. The obstinacy of your enemies is so fierce that peace and arbitration with them is utterly impossible." This is how each day must begin. Immediately, upon awakening, "consider yourself as on the field of battle, facing the enemy and bound by the iron-clad law—either fight or die."[34] Now how is it possible for the Christian soldier, continuously confronted with the harsh reality imposed by such a "law," ever to achieve anything resembling peace of mind? Scupoli's answer to this question was straightforward: God delights in the battle, approves of it, and "encourages everyone to engage in it." But the divine victory is assured. In the end, God will triumph. If one places one's trust entirely in God, no matter how overwhelming the enemy may appear, victory is assured.

Nothing should be allowed to disturb this peace of mind. It is a great shield that the enemy cannot penetrate. Scupoli devoted his twenty-fifth chapter to a discussion of its importance. "Without it, your pious exercises will be fruitless. I am convinced that, if the heart is troubled, the enemy is ever able to strike us, and as much as he wishes. Moreover, in that state we are not capable of discerning the true path to follow, the snares that must be avoided to attain virtue."[35] Once again, the argument takes on a semiotic character, because peace of mind is required for discernment, for an accurate interpretation of human experience. On Scupoli's account, this peace is not something that can be neatly distinguished from a habit of detachment and the power of self-control. These are all related aspects of the same spiritual ideal, the complex disposition of a dedicated Christian soldier.

Toward the end of the book, Scupoli turned to prayer, the final and also the most important weapon in the Christian's spiritual arsenal. "Prayer is the channel of all divine grace; by it, God is compelled, as it were, to grant us the strength of heaven, and destroy by our weak hands the fiercest of our foes."[36] In a series of chapters, Scupoli treated the different forms of prayer, vocal and mental prayer, as well as various methods of meditation. The prescribed meditations, as in many of Ignatius's exercises, are consistently focused on the life, teaching, and suffering of Christ, the last of these taking on a special significance for the person seeking guidance and inspiration in the spiritual combat. A distinctive feature of some of the methods outlined by Scupoli is the corporate sensibility that they evoke. The enemy takes many forms and employs a variety of tactics: sensuality (chapter 13), sudden passions (chapter 18), sloth (chapter 20), delusions (chapter 23), spiritual dryness (chapter 59), fear of death (chapter 61), despair (chapter 64), and vainglory (chapter 65). An individual might be overwhelmed by this attack on multiple fronts, but no one ought to engage in the fight alone. Christ is the principal ally as well as the commander-in-chief in this campaign. Several of the methods of meditation also describe how the Virgin Mary and an entire army of saints and angels might be enlisted for support (chapters 49 and 50).

Prayer was given a certain primacy in Scupoli's analysis not because it is superior to the other strategies but because it incorporates and perfects them. It is the most effective means for achieving distrust of self and confidence in God, for ordering the human faculties. Its end is complete conformity of the human will to the divine will so that everything is undertaken for the greater glory of God. On this view, Christian prayer is governed by the same logic of self-forgetfulness already encountered in the examination of spiritual exercises from a variety of religious traditions. If its practice is persistent, it should result for the one who prays in the attainment of a certain state of emptiness. Toward the end of his treatise, Scupoli sketched a meditation appropriate for the period of time immediately after receiving the Eucharist. The communicant is to inquire of the Lord, "O eternal love, what is it you ask of me?" And the Lord will reply: "Will nothing, think nothing, understand nothing, see nothing but Me and My will. Let thy nothingness be lost in the depths of My infinity, and find there thy happiness, as I find repose in thee."[37]

The spiritual legacy of Saint Antony of the Desert was later to become embodied in the tradition of *hesychasm* within Orthodox Christianity. Here is a method of prayer closely resembling the practice of dhikr in Islam, with some striking similarities to Hindu yoga and the discipline of zazen. The term derives from the Greek word *hesychia*, meaning quiet. It is an ancient method of Christian prayer employing the frequent repetition of the name of Jesus and the use of controlled breathing to focus attention and effect a state of tranquility.

The thirteenth-century Orthodox theologian Gregory Palamas represented this hesychastic tradition and defended it against its critics. He reported the teachings of spiritual masters who advised that a person, when praying, should not allow the eye to "roam hither and thither" but instead "fix it on his breast or on his navel, as a point of concentration." It is for the same purpose of controlling distracting thoughts and impulses that one is instructed also to employ basic techniques of breathing.

This is why certain masters recommend them to control the movement inwards and outwards of the breath, and to hold it back a little; in this way, they will also be able to control the mind together with the breath—this, at any rate, until such time as they have made progress, with the aid of God, have restrained the intellect from becoming distracted by what surrounds it, have purified it and truly become capable of leading it to a "unified recollection." One can state that this recollection is a spontaneous effect of the attention of the mind, for the to-and-fro movement of breath becomes quieted during intensive reflection, especially with those who maintain inner quiet in body and soul.[38]

The settling of attention in the center of the body, the regulation of breathing, and the repetition of a mantra like the Jesus Prayer ("Lord Jesus Christ Son of God, have mercy on me a sinner") are all practices that link hesychasm to various forms of spiritual exercise in other religions. Yet for the purposes of this analysis, the most important connection is the one established by the continued emphasis in hesychasm on the martial significance of these techniques.

If not always stressed quite to the extent that it was for Antony and his brothers in the desert, the challenge of the spiritual combat was certainly never ignored by these later masters. Gregory was careful to interpret Saint Paul's teaching on the body as indicating that it is *not* to be regarded as something intrinsically evil. Nevertheless, it is a potential locus of evil, a place that can readily become occupied and corrupted by evil influences, so that one must struggle to drive the "law of sin" out of the body and replace it with the power of a "watchful" mind, a quiet heart.[39]

The Protestant reformers understood themselves to be engaged in an intense spiritual struggle, much as Catholic reformers like Ignatius of Loyola and Lorenzo Scupoli did. The deployment of explicitly martial categories to portray the spiritual life is a practice that waxes and wanes during different historical periods and varies from theologian to theologian. The great American Calvinist Jonathan Edwards understood the spiritual life as an ongoing battle with satanic forces. He formulated a complex semiotic analysis of the cues supplied by human experience for the purpose of the discernment of spirits.[40] In a manner reminiscent of Ignatius, Edwards portrayed Satan as an enemy who frequently acts surreptitiously, in disguise, working to inspire false confidence and a sense of ease. Prayerful vigilance, disciplined self-criticism, hope of and trust in God's grace, and the cultivation of virtue in Christian practice are the most effective means for resisting this enemy.

Early in the twentieth century, the ascetical theologian Adolphe Tanquerey summarized classical Roman Catholic perspectives on the interior combat in his famous treatise on spirituality.[41] Echoing the medieval scholastics, Tanquerey depicted the "higher faculties" of intellect and will as being impervious to the direct attacks of the devil: "God has kept these as a sanctuary for Himself, and He alone can enter there and touch the mainspring of the will without doing violence to it." The body and its appetites, however, are vulnerable to the enemy's influences, as are the imagination and memory. This is where evil does its primary work so that the will is affected indirectly through the body and the lower faculties. The spiritual combat, thus portrayed, is an exercise of freedom, the flexing of the soul's volitional musculature in defending and maintaining control over the more vulnerable aspects of the self.

In most modern Christian theology of the spiritual life, however, there is a dramatically diminished emphasis on talk about evil spirits and spiritual warfare, on the use of martial images to portray the challenges confronting practitioners who engage in the regular discipline of prayer and meditation. Lingering Gnostic attitudes concerning the body and the physical senses as sources of corruption have been gradually softened and neutralized. An oppressively negative Augustinian theology of human sexuality and concupiscence, with its discernment of a dark sin-fulness poisoning natural human desires, has been gradually transcended (even in some traditional Christian churches that continue to maintain quite conservative perspectives on issues of sexual morality). Colorful descriptions of demonic forces in-vading the soul have been replaced by modern psychological analyses of internal conflict; these are linked to therapeutic strategies of resolution that have supplanted the older military tactics. The discourse of a martial spirituality has not evaporated altogether, but to the extent that it survives within modern Chris-tian theology it tends to be interpreted in essentially metaphori-cal terms.

A disinclination to perceive the body or "flesh" as an enemy can easily be defended as a healthy development within modern Christian spirituality. It reduces the possibility of a masochistic, self-destructive asceticism being evaluated as an acceptable form of spiritual discipline. And it has made possible the appropria-tion by Christian practitioners of techniques of meditation de-veloped in other religious traditions, traditions like Daoism that understand the cultivation of the body as playing a positive role in spiritual development. Despite certain discernible Gnostic tendencies manifested in its history, Christianity in its more or-thodox forms has always refused to embrace the perspective that matter and the body are essentially evil. From Antony to Tan-querey, the key assumption has been that the body and its ap-petites are most vulnerable to seduction, most easily corrupted, stressing the need for vigilance, discipline, and self-control.

What might be sacrificed or lost within Christianity if the tradition of martial spirituality were to be extinguished alto-gether—if all talk about the spiritual combat were to cease? That question, not restricted to a discussion of Christian perspectives, will receive more extended treatment in the final chapter, but some vague hypotheses can at least be sketched here. One of the roles conceivably played by the theology of the spiritual combat is its functioning as a safeguard against spiritual discipline becoming excessively individualistic. As traditionally articulated, this theology describes the combat as participation in a cosmic struggle. Even when the enemy is encountered in the psyche's most private recesses, it represents an evil that transcends the self, a ubiquitous, pervasive force in the world. Martial spirituality cannot easily be reduced to a comfortable exercise in self-absorption. Its wisdom cannot be purchased as the investment in some convenient and effective form of spiritual technology. It demands courage, heroic self-sacrifice, and strenuous self-discipline. It constitutes a strategy of resistance to an evil perceived as real and really threatening. In focusing attention on the self, it seeks to develop the interpretive skill required for understanding the world that lies beyond the self, the resources for surviving its challenges and temptations.

One school of modern Christian thought that has not ignored or suppressed martial categories is liberation theology. Here the recognition of real evil and injustice in the world and of the Christian duty of resistance has operated as the key insight needing theological explication and application. Moreover, it is interesting to observe that the type of spirituality most typically linked to such liberation perspectives is one that represents the human body in generally positive terms—conceives of persons as being essentially and not accidentally *embodied* spirits.[42] At the same time, there has been little attempt on the part of liberation thinkers to exploit the rich resources of the traditional theology of the spiritual combat. Martial images drawn from Christian scriptures, especially from the literature of the Old Testament, have been effectively utilized by these thinkers. But the vast body of material on prayer and meditation, on its character as a form of struggle or resistance, has not been so commonly exploited for its possible relevance to specific political, social or ethical issues.

Any attempt to recover that traditional perspective runs its own risks, for all of the same reasons that the modern developments in Christian ascetical theology cited above can be praised as healthy ones. Attentiveness to styles of martial spirituality in non-Christian religions (a project initiated here) might offer one means of counterbalancing the more problematic aspects of Christian asceticism, protecting against the revival of heavily Gnostic influences, for example. At the same time, one should not neglect to observe those counterbalances and safeguards that are already a part of the tradition. A brief mention of some of these will supply a useful transition to the philosophical discussion that follows.

If the enemy is real and the spiritual "combat" represents a genuine conflict, nevertheless, it should be noted (as with Ueshiba, so, too, within Christianity) that love is the primary mode of resistance. This begins with the love of God, to be sure, with complete devotion to God and surrender to the divine will, but Christians must also make sense out of Jesus' difficult teaching that they are to love their enemies. The power of this love is a peculiar power, because it is effective to the degree that it consists in one's recognizing and declaring one's own powerlessness. Initially, as Scupoli insisted, this takes the form of a complete distrust of self, an awareness of one's impotence in the face of an overwhelming evil. Yet confidence is to be placed in one whose power is displayed most perfectly (according to Saint Paul) in his apparent powerlessness on the cross. Identification with the mind of Christ is a process, then, that deepens rather than softens this paradoxical understanding of what it means to be powerful.

The tradition is consistent in its assumption that the essence of freedom is a habit of detachment, essential for the achievement of even the smallest measure of self-control. Now this control can be understood (and often has been) in an oppressively hierarchical fashion as involving the mastery of the "higher" elements of the self over the "lower," the necessary hegemony of "spirit" over "flesh." But it does not seem essential that self-control be construed in this fashion, that the spiritual combat be localized in such a manner. Charles Peirce's philosophy will supply an alternative conceptual scheme for the theological articulation of what such a freedom entails. It does not require pitting the higher against the lower, but rather represents the self in contemplation as exercising a more gentle influence over future conduct through a process of habit formation.

FIVE

Toward a Moral Equivalent of War

In his 1910 essay "The Moral Equivalent of War," William James argued that a successful pacifism must reject the typical goals and methods of human warfare, while nevertheless seeking to incorporate and adapt certain martial virtues and disciplines. The notion that war is "good for nothing" is one that James regarded as naïve and unperceptive. His concern was not with an assessment of the sort of rationale or objectives typically established for military campaigns (i.e., not with an evaluation of those moral conditions under which some war could be judged a "just war"); rather, his interest was in the pragmatic effects of military training and combat on those who engage in such activities. These effects, while not entirely epiphenomenal, would rarely be identified as the primary purpose for engaging in an actual conflict. Nevertheless, they are essential ingredients of the "aesthetical and ethical point of view" articulated by "reflective apologists" for war in general—that is, those who claim that the waging of war, whatever its risks and potential destructiveness, is an activity vital to the health of human individuals and societies.

James took such apologists seriously precisely because he valued the qualities that contribute to success in combat. These included, on his reckoning, fidelity, tenacity, intrepidity, heroism, conscience, inventiveness, physical health and vigor, and the surrender of private interest.[1] Not only do they lead to success in combat, moreover, these capacities are tested, exercised, and so enhanced, by the conflict itself. The challenge for pacifists, then, was to propose an effective "substitute for war's disciplinary function," as James conceived of it, "a moral equivalent of war."[2]

James sketched such a proposal in the latter half of his essay, calling for the conscription of an "army enlisted against Nature."[3] However infelicitous this talk about "human warfare with nature" may now appear, the basic idea that inspired it is nonetheless worthy of consideration. If war among human beings were "the only force that can discipline a whole community," James concluded, "then war must have its way." But he envisioned the possibility of an "equivalent discipline":

The martial type of character can be bred without war. Strenuous honor and disinterestedness abound elsewhere. Priests and medical men are in a fashion educated to it, and we should feel some degree of it imperative if we were conscious of our work as an obligatory service to the state. We should be *owned*, as soldiers are by the army, and our pride would rise accordingly. We could be poor, then, without humiliation, as army officers now are. The only thing needed henceforward is to inflame the civic temper as past history has inflamed the military temper.[4]

James's pacifism was rooted in his conviction that the martial character can be bred "without war." Toward this end, he conceived and advocated another type of warfare: a new breed of soldier would be enlisted to combat and subdue a very different kind of enemy, here, the hostile forces of "nature." These "soldiers" would be summoned to "coal and iron mines, to freight trains, to fishing fleets in December, to dishwashing, clotheswashing, and window-washing, to road-building and tunnelmaking, to foundries and stoke-holes, and to the frames of skyscrapers."[5] Their service would be temporary, but as a consequence of it they would "come back into society with healthier sympathies and soberer ideas."

James recognized that the fear of a hostile other can indeed be a spur to the development of certain distinctive virtues, an impetus to self-discipline. At the same time, he cautioned that it is an error to regard this sort of fear as "the only stimulus known for awakening the higher ranges of men's spiritual energy."[6]

Whatever the stimulus, this process of "awakening" was the primary focus of James's concern. As a pragmatist, his interest was in the effects of combat—especially, in this instance, its transformative effects on the combatants. James identified these changes as the development in youth of a sense of loyalty and devotion to ideals, a strengthening of the will, the breeding of civic mindedness, and a spirit of disinterestedness. It is possible, he argued, to obtain those effects while simultaneously eliminating the hatefulness, destructiveness, and cruelty of war. The potential consequences for human social life are equally positive and desirable; that is to say, it is possible to banish "the gory nurse that trained societies to cohesiveness" and yet still continue to build cohesive societies.

In an essay written only a few years earlier, James had concluded that, "compared with what we ought to be, we are only half awake."[7] There, already, he was struck by "examples of how war will wake a man up," releasing energies hitherto untapped and unobserved. It will do so because the "excitement" and emotions that are aroused by war are powerful "inciters of the will." Unfortunately, once removed from the excitement of combat, "the shallower levels of life tend to close in and shut us off";[8] consequently, it has become necessary to develop a "methodical ascetical discipline" to keep the deeper levels of freedom and power of will "constantly in reach." In that essay, James briefly discussed the Hindu practice of yoga as the primary example of such a discipline, but he also suspected that "Ignatius Loyola's spiritual exercises must have produced this result in innumerable devotees."

The example of Ignatius's exercises is noteworthy here primarily because they are identified as an *alternative* to the excitement of war as a means of awakening human energies, of testing and strengthening volition. Yet Ignatius understood his Christian exercitants to be engaged in the preparation for a *real* combat—one with exceedingly dark and threatening spiritual forces. So James, at the same time that he seemed to have discovered

an alternative to war, anticipated his later discussion, propos-
ing also an "equivalent" for war. These considerations blend
with his discussion of the power that certain ideas have to "naturally awaken the energies of loyalty, courage, endurance, or devotion."[9] If an ascetic discipline can be conceived not simply as
an alternative to military training but, rather, as itself constituting a form of military activity, then its power to excite emotions
and motivate the will is enhanced. Here, what is added to the ascetic practice is the *idea* of war. On this view, spiritual practice is
always already a martial discipline; at the same time, the idea of
war is itself transformed, as the concept of enemy and strategies
for fighting must be reformulated.

Almost a decade before he published his essay on "moral
war," James had already addressed the same topic in his Gifford
Lectures *The Varieties of Religious Experience.* "One hears of the
mechanical equivalent of heat. What we now need to discover in
the social realm is the moral equivalent of war; something heroic
that will speak to men as war does, and yet will be compatible
with their spiritual selves as war has proved itself to be incom-
patible."[10] The context for these remarks was one of his lectures
on "The Value of Saintliness." That context suggests (notwithstanding the peculiar shape taken by the later essay's call for a
"war against nature") that the roots of this idea of an equivalent
for war can be traced to James's deliberations concerning specifically religious topics.

Indeed, here it was linked to a discussion of ascetic practices—to a pragmatic assessment of their contemporary significance. Despite the possibility of excesses that violate common
sense (the "uselessness of some of the particular acts" that can be
associated with asceticism) James felt that the "general good intention" of asceticism was of sufficient value "to rehabilitate it in
our esteem." "For in its spiritual meaning asceticism stands for
nothing less than for the essence of the twice-born philosophy.
It symbolizes . . . the belief that there is an element of real
wrongness in the world, which is neither to be ignored or

evaded, but which must be squarely met and overcome by an appeal to the soul's heroic resources, and neutralized and cleansed away by suffering."[11]

This reference to the "twice-born philosophy" recalled James's earlier lectures on the religious perspective of the "sick soul," as contrasted with the "healthy-minded" philosophy. In the latter, peace is conceived as something "reached by the simple addition of pluses and the elimination of minuses from life." But for the sick soul, every natural good is false "in its very being." "Canceled as it all is by death, if not by earlier enemies, it gives no final balance, and can never be the thing intended for our lasting worship. It keeps us from our real good, rather; and renunciation and despair of it are our first step in the direction of truth. There are two lives, the natural and the spiritual, and we must lose the one before we can participate in the other."[12] The natural optimism of the healthy-minded perspective is purchased at the price of a blindness to the truth. Suffering is unavoidable. Evil is real. Death is inevitable. There is a "real wrongness in the world" that ought to be confronted squarely and resisted by every means possible.

In order to take this "first step" toward the truth, James called for the abandonment of a "fear of poverty"; indeed, he advocated a positive embracing of poverty, much as soldiers can be poor "without humiliation." James's extended consideration of this topic revealed that his primary interest was in something akin to what theologians refer to as a "poverty of spirit"; he pointed to Jesuit priests, Muslim dervishes, Hindu fakirs, and Buddhist monks as being exemplary in this regard. What James judged to be primarily problematic was not the mere legal possession of property but, more fundamentally, psychic attachment to worldly goods and values. Spiritual poverty, he concluded, was a cultivated disposition toward possessions, rather than a simple lack of them, a "having all things as though one did not have them" (to paraphrase Saint Paul). "In short, lives based on having are less free than lives based on doing or on being, and in the interest of action people subject to spiritual excitement throw away possessions as so many clogs. Only those who have no private interests can follow an ideal straight away."[13]

Here is a type of freedom that James felt most of his contemporaries were unable even to imagine. This "liberation from material attachments" he characterized as "the manlier indifference"; a person thus disposed was in "the moral fighting shape." This "moral fighting" differs from war in the ordinary sense, not least of all because it is rational and requires of its warriors a supreme self-control, whereas the latter is the "wholesale organization of irrationality," an activity primarily aimed at savagery and destruction.[14]

It would be a mistake to reduce James's argument here to the claim that, for a person who is properly disposed, war can be considered as "moral"—that is, under those conditions human conflict can be morally justified. His insight cuts deeper than that. James concluded that the whole of spiritual life, morality itself, can be conceived in martial terms. In one of the earliest lectures from the *Varieties* he announced that

for morality life is a war, and the service of the highest is a kind of cosmic patriotism, which also calls for volunteers. Even a sick man, unable to be militant outwardly, can carry on the moral warfare. He can willfully turn his attention away from his own future, whether in this world or the next. He can train himself to indifference to his present drawbacks and immerse himself in whatever objective interests still remain accessible. . . . Such a man lives on his loftiest, highest plane. He is a high-hearted freeman and no pining slave."[15]

Training to indifference is primarily an exercise of volition on James's account. It is all a matter of how one pays attention since "volition [will] is nothing but attention."[16] One chooses to pay attention, or, more accurately, one chooses the amount of effort with which to pay attention to whatever attracts one's interest. This choosing-the-amount-of-effort-in-attending is the way that persons manifest their freedom. Religion and morality, as well as an individual's sense of self-worth, are rooted in the ability to make such choices. Moreover, the process of choosing is ongoing, a continuous struggle to decide what matters most and to resist distraction. That is how individuals shape the kind of world they inhabit and the sorts of persons they will become in the future. It is the essence of self-control, requiring the kind of discipline and heroic effort that James frequently portrayed as martial virtues. Here again, even if there is real evil in the world, the primary conflict takes place on an interior battleground within the self.

Choices occur not only with respect to what one does but also in response to what one experiences, even in instances when one has no control over what is happening. One can assent or not assent to things as they occur, pay more or less attention to them, as well as control the quality of one's attention. Now to some, what one adds by consenting to something that happens willy-nilly may seem to be negligible; it may seem a fairly trivial exercise of freedom. But to James it made all the difference in the world whether one lived one's life deliberately or got swept along in a meaningless chain of events.

It is possible to read James's philosophy in such a way that the pragmatic meaning of *enemy* is supplied precisely in terms of effects wrought both within the self and among selves. There is no fixed sense of the term; there is a conventional meaning, perhaps, but no single definition of the word from a pragmatic perspective. If one's response to enemies is, for example, a loving response, then enemies effectively cease to be enemies. As Ueshiba suggested, there are opponents everywhere, "but actually there is no opponent there." This does not mean that courage is any less required; one might need a tremendous amount of courage in order to maintain a spirit of reconciliation in the face of hostility. Moreover, the self-control that is prerequisite for such a loving response might be maintained only with great fortitude: control over one's violent feelings of anger, one's pride, one's own lust to dominate or to humiliate another, might be achieved only with a fierce determination. In James's view, the love of enemies represents a power so extraordinary that it "might conceivably transform the world." To succeed in cultivating this love as a disposition "would involve such a breach with our instinctive springs of action as a whole, and with the present world's arrangements, that a critical point would practically be passed, and we should be born into another kingdom of being. Religious emotion makes us feel that other kingdom to be close at hand, within our reach."[17]

It is important to recognize that the saint's struggle to transform the self through asceticism has broad implications of a public, social nature. One must always consider the dangerous potential of spiritual practices to become privatistic and self-absorbed. Yet despite his emphasis on the intensely private character of all religious experience, James's primary concern was with both the personal and public "fruits" of asceticism. Moreover, to conceive of religious discipline as a martial activity could be interpreted as a way to reduce the risk of spiritual solipsism. The martial virtues that James celebrated, while they were to be inculcated in individuals, all had a social or civic utility. It was not, for James, simply a matter of pretending that there are enemies to fight and then playing at make-believe war in order to discipline the character and will of persons in their solitude. Rather, he was convinced that there are real problems in the world, evils "neither to be ignored or evaded," and only properly disciplined persons will be capable of meeting the challenge that they represent.

It is also hard to imagine how the spiritual life, conceived as a form of combat, could represent a shrinking from public concerns and moral responsibility when such a conception emphasizes (as it surely did for James) a heroic detachment from private interests and personal inclinations. The traumatic influence of war is such that it can both require and inspire that type of disinterestedness, even "unto death." In a complex variety of senses, war is all about death—the death of each person, the death of each moment that passes in time, the dying to self, the sacrificial dying for another. The specter of death haunted James's "sick soul" as the ultimate threat to the meaning of life, surpassing all "earlier enemies" yet making the spiritual life possible. One must "stare death right in the face," Ueshiba warned, "in order to illumine the Path."

James believed that when the experience of meaning occurs in the spiritual life, it often appears as a *gift* "from sources sometimes high and sometimes low" and almost always "beyond our control."[18] Death itself can be the bearer of such a gift. Just as the drowsy person is jolted to full consciousness by the sound of gunfire or the rumble of an earthquake, the confrontation with death in spiritual practice can precipitate an awakening. That awakening can be either sudden or gradual; it can take the form of a deeper self-awareness or it can manifest itself as a power to discern another person's joy or suffering. Though it can be struggled for, even fought for, the fruits of that awakening can nevertheless seem gratuitous, therefore, as something to be both celebrated in gratitude and communicated generously to others.

William James was one of Charles Peirce's closest friends, and the two men shared a number of important philosophical and personal perspectives. Peirce's life and family seem to have been less dramatically affected by the tragedy of the Civil War than the Jameses, and Peirce less frequently employed a martial vocabulary in his writings. But though he devoted less energy than James to a consideration of the martial virtues,[19] he clearly regarded human life as a struggle, a contest requiring of its participants both a heroic indifference and a supreme self-control. There are a great many reasons why Peirce may have been inclined to adopt such a view. Not only did he write and think in the wake of the Civil War but he was also part of an intellectual community that wrestled in the late nineteenth century with the ideas of Charles Darwin and evolutionism. Darwin portrayed the natural environment as an arena of conflict for organisms struggling to adapt to its changing features and competing with one another for the limited resources that it supplied. Within such an arena, only the strongest individuals will flourish and only the fittest will survive.

Now Peirce could hardly ignore the principle of natural selection as Darwin articulated it, but he believed that its importance as an explanation for the process of evolution had been greatly exaggerated. It was not in competition with other individuals but in the competition to eliminate a narrow individualism that Peirce saw the real battle as being enjoined. His was a religious perspective on evolution, a perspective that supplied the rationale for Peirce's own peculiar brand of martial spirituality:

A religious organization is a somewhat idle affair unless it be sworn in as a regiment of that great army that takes life in hand, with all its delights, in grimmest fight to put down the principle of self-seeking, and to make the principle of love triumphant. It has something more serious to think about than the phraseology of the articles of war. Fall into the ranks then; follow your colonel. Keep your one purpose steadily and alone in view, and you may promise yourself the attainment of your sole desire, which is to hasten the chariot wheels of redeeming love![20]

There is a complex cosmological story to be told about Peirce's theory of evolution as "agapism," in some ways similar to the Daoist narrative about how all particular things in their heterogeneous differences have first emerged, then developed, from out of a state of primordial chaos and emptiness.[21] But attention must be focused here more narrowly on the discipline required of each person who aspires in some small way to contribute to the creative work of evolutionary love. The essence of that discipline, with all the martial virtues that it entails, is most clearly exposed in Peirce's philosophical reflections concerning the nature and importance of self-control.[22]

Now one of the more poignant features of Charles Peirce's biography is the importance he attached to self-control, both as a personal quality and as a philosophical concept, even though he was convinced that the lack of it was his most desperate character flaw. In a later commentary on one of his earliest published essays, Peirce characterized self-control as involving a "love of what is good for all on the whole."[23] He identified it with the "essence of Christianity" and described it as "perfect freedom," indeed, as "the only freedom of which man has any reason to be proud." Yet Peirce was not at all proud of possessing what he judged to be insufficient "moral self-control," a failing for which he at least partially blamed his father.[24] While Benjamin Peirce took great pains to challenge his son intellectually, he apparently neglected to discipline him in other respects. Charles was to remark from the perspective of his later years that as a youth he "was brought up with far too loose a rein."[25] Not all of the dark secrets in Peirce's life have been exposed; but some of the tragic personal consequences of his inability to control his behavior— his temper, his sexual impulse, his use of intoxicants, and his incautious spending of money—have been well-documented.

References to self-control as a virtue have been ubiquitous in this discussion of martial spirituality. But what does it mean to control the "self"? Exactly whom or what is one attempting to control, and who does the controlling? How is this accomplished? How does one fail to accomplish it? In what way does an act of self-control differ from control exerted over someone else, or over objects and events in the world? How can the exercise of self-control be conceived as the most effective means for controlling others? Conversely, is it possible to surrender oneself to the will of another while still maintaining self-control, the "perfect freedom" that Peirce described as "service to Christ"?

These questions constitute a starting point for inquiry; the search for answers is a task that can only be initiated here. This much does seem clear. Self-control is a matter of deliberate, rational behavior, of thinking, choosing, and then acting on one's choices, all of which takes time. So one of the ways to approach the question of "who controls whom?" is to conceive of the one who controls as acting upon some future version of the self. Even in cases where one struggles in the "here and now" to control some powerful impulse or desire, a process of deliberation is taking place, however hasty and desperate it may be, in the attempt to control the immediate future. If desire proceeds unchecked to motivate conduct, if one acts impulsively, then the battle is already lost before any element of self-control can be brought into play.

It is possible, of course, to think about self-control as something that one exercises in the moment, that is, at the very moment when one is confronted by some temptation or moved to act in a way contrary to one's ideals, one's best judgment. One is able to overcome the present urge to act in anger, for example, perhaps because of the predictable negative consequences of such behavior (raising one's blood pressure, endangering a friendship, the possibility of retaliation, etc.) or because such behavior violates some code of moral or social propriety. Similarly, one politely refuses the cocktail now being offered by a host, after a quick calculation concerning level of fatigue, alcohol already consumed, and the long ride home. Here is a form of freedom or of self-control manifested as a decision, as a particular act of choosing in the present moment. But notice that even in this form, self-control presupposes a kind of dialogue (sometimes precipitating a conflict) between the present self and the self that will act in the immediate future. Furthermore, it can often entail deliberations requiring a person imaginatively to conceive of the distant future, of the remote effects and long-term consequences of behavior.

Peirce himself did not tend to think of self-control as a form of freedom most perfectly manifested in specific acts of volition, of deciding either to refrain from doing what one judges to be wrong or to do the right thing. On his account, self-control operates at a distance, shaping particular future actions and deci-

sions indirectly by working more immediately to effect specific changes within the self. It is primarily an exercise in habit
formation, sometimes also a matter of dissolving old habits
deemed inappropriate or ineffective, of eradicating vices. On such
a view, that person is most free who does the right thing at any
given moment without having, in some heroic act of volitional
exertion, to subdue temptations or overcome moral inertia. This
freedom is experienced as a kind of ease in action, rather than as
a deliberate choosing; but in fact it will be rooted in a whole series of deliberate choices that one has made about the sort of person that one wants to be or to become.

On this Peircean view, "the power of self-control is certainly
not a power over what one is doing at the very instant the operation of self-control is commenced."[26] It is more appropriately
conceived as the general form that a person gives to his or her life
and actions, the gradual "building up a character."[27] It is the "capacity for rising to an extended view of a practical subject instead
of seeing only temporary urgency."[28] Freedom exercised in this
way will impart to future actions a "fixed character . . . measured
by the absence of the feeling of self-reproach."[29]

This general Peircean perspective is one that is useful for understanding the sort of martial character that practitioners might
struggle to develop in a variety of meditative traditions. It incorporates a semiotic view of the self; that is, the idea of the self as
a continuous stream of semiosis, a "living inferential metaboly
of symbols." As such, the self is engaged in the ongoing interpretation of itself to itself. Insofar as this process is deliberate
and self-controlled, it will acquire a certain general character, so
that "the *vir* is begotten."[30] To be a self, in this particular sense, is
both to have ideals (including specifically religious ideals) and
gradually to embody these ideals through the development of
appropriate habits, thus shaping future conduct, imparting to it
a discernible form and consistency. One can, first, conceive of
such ideals as symbols and then see the specific habits of conduct as the interpretations (what Peirce called "interpretants")

of those symbols. Consequently, persons or selves are complex symbols, and their meaning is displayed in the consistency of self-controlled behavior.[31] As the earlier investigation of the martial arts has indicated, self-interpretation is a process intimately related to the task of understanding the intentions and behavior of others. Moreover, the self-controlled formation of the "vir" can include the development of bodily habits of posture, breathing, and movement, not merely alongside the practice of cultivating spiritual and moral dispositions but in a way that is integrally connected to it.

Meditative disciplines are most often designed to transform human awareness, as well as to shape a person's typical feeling responses to the elements of her or his experience. Yet perceptions and emotions, at least on a quick first inspection, appear to be the sorts of things over which one has very little control. Seeing the ladder leaning against the wall, for example, is not a matter of deciding what one wants to see or deliberating about what one ought to see. If one is looking at the ladder, paying attention, and the view is not obscured, then one just sees it. Of course, Peirce contributed as much as any other modern philosopher to the project of undermining those varieties of empiricism grounded in the problematic assumption that we "just see" things. Perceptual judgments are forms of hypothetical (what Peirce called "abductive") inference; these inferences can be faulty so that they ought to be subjected to critical scrutiny. But the key point here is that, as inferences, they are unconscious, immediate, and largely uncontrollable.

A similar view of feelings and emotions can be articulated. People (and especially martial artists) talk about the importance of "controlling their emotions." But the point of such talk often seems to be to underscore the necessity of not acting rashly on the basis of what one feels. One can control what one does in a way that one cannot control what one feels, so that it might seem excessively scrupulous to submit emotions to the same sort of moral evaluation that one's actions are required to undergo.

On any theory of self-control that limits its exercise to acts of volition performed in the present moment, it would be reasonable to conclude that perceptions and emotions are not subject to a great deal of self-control; but that is not the Peircean view being sketched here. It is possible to argue that both how one perceives something and what one feels in a given situation are morally meaningful phenomena, vulnerable to criticism. One's ideals about the sort of person one ought to become guide the deliberate process of shaping the self into just such a person. Perceptions and emotions are interpretive responses to persons, things, and events that, while they may be largely uncontrollable at the moment of their occurrence, can be dramatically shaped in the long run by those habits of thought and feeling that one chooses to inculcate.

It may take more than a little bit of brainwashing for a person to learn not to see the ladder as a ladder. But one might be able to train oneself to see snow in the way that an Eskimo sees it or to hear music in the way that one's music teacher does. Whatever else one might conclude about such examples, they are not obviously instances of "brainwashing." In the same way, one's feeling responses to things can be modified over time through the controlled formation of new habitual responses, so that someone might learn to enjoy rather than to fear riding on a roller-coaster or develop a genuine sympathy and affection for a person previously disdained. Moreover, religiously meaningful experiences, religious feelings and perceptions, are nourished by habits of interpretation that may be more or less well developed in any given individual.[32] One has to be the sort of person who would tend to experience things and situations in just such a religiously meaningful fashion. (This observation does not settle the debate about whether or not it is always a good thing to be that sort of person.) In any event, the development of habits is a process that can to some extent be controlled—by others seeking to shape one's behavior, of course, but also by oneself.[33]

To affirm that self-control involves a process of habit formation is not yet to say very much about how that process typically unfolds or about the variety of possible strategies designed to facilitate the process. (There must be strategies, after all, if the strengthening of habits is to be considered a deliberate and rational process; that is, a kind of practice.) Already it is possible, however, to comment about what it means for a person either to succeed or to fail in exercising self-control. If *"ought* implies *can,"* then it might seem implausible to argue that a person ought to perceive or feel or act in a way that is precluded by that person's present dispositions and capabilities. But on the view that the properly self-controlled person will take responsibility for the development of dispositions and capabilities deemed necessary for appropriate future conduct, talk about failure (or about "defeat" from a martial point of view) does not seem out of line.

It is inevitable, of course, no matter how well-disciplined a person might be, that she or he will experience contingencies that could not be predicted in advance, situations that may challenge her or his power of self-control. Such a case will require the flexing of sheer volitional muscle right on the spot if the present challenge is to be overcome. Nevertheless, this muscle, this willpower, is also the kind of thing that one might be able to exercise and develop over time. And so while it is reasonable to conclude that maintaining self-control is not always easy, it is important to observe that the difficulty will be considerably greater for the person who never prepares for or thinks about the future.

A great deal of that sort of preparation, Peirce believed, takes place in the imagination. Indeed, the highest grade of self-control, on his account, is achieved when a person can "control his self-control. When this point is reached, much or all of the training will be conducted in the imagination."[34] It is the type of training that involves the deliberate formation of habits of action by imagining a particular kind of occasion as a "stimulus" and then thinking about what the consequences of various actions performed in the situation would be. Some of these will be endorsed as appropriate, given their compatibility with the ideals and values of the person doing the imagining. Repeated imaginings, Peirce conjectured, will dispose a person actually to perform the right action when such an occasion arises. Peirce concluded that giving this "general shape to our actual future conduct is what we call a *resolve.*"[35]

Systems of religious meditation display an intricate logic that no brief account could unravel; furthermore, that logic varies with differing systems. But Peirce's discussion of a kind of training in self-control that takes place through the exercise of the imagination supplies an important semiotic perspective on at least some of those religious practices. In isolation, his ideas about the effect that repeated imaginings will have on future behavior are too vague to be anything more than suggestive. They need to be supplemented by an account of what happens whenever one pays *attention* to anything at all, whether in the imagination or in one's everyday experience of the world.

Meditation has been portrayed throughout this discussion as a discipline of attention. It is a process of deliberation that differs from other forms of reasoning in that it is explicitly designed to be self-reflexive and self-transforming. Here is a prescribed method of thinking about things, of paying attention to them, in a way intended to produce in the thinker new habits of thought, feeling, and action. Paying attention, in itself, may seem like an easy thing to do if one just decides to do it, a task not involving any special skill or training. But experience shows that it can be extraordinarily difficult to accomplish. One may intend to pay attention to X, only to find oneself repeatedly distracted, soon confessing like Saint Paul did that, despite one's best intentions, "I cannot do it."[36] When the object of attention is of great importance and the interfering distractions are numerous and lively, the struggle to attend can take on the characteristics of a fierce battle (as in the spiritual combat). The precise nature of this conflict deserves more extended philosophical consideration.

One's attention may be aroused by something because it is interesting. Yet Peirce also observed that one can generate interest in something by the fact of paying attention to it: attention increases the "subjective intensity" of one's consciousness of a thing. This is a "temporary condition"; that is, the intensity will soon diminish, but only because the idea of that thing will become linked in consciousness to other ideas, acquiring a greater generality and, thus, an ability to determine conduct.[37] Consider Peirce's analysis: "This is what constitutes the fixation of attention. Contemplation consists in our using our self-control to remove us from the forcible intrusion of other thoughts, and in considering the interesting bearings of what may lie hidden in the icon, so as to cause the subjective intensity of it to increase."[38]

Attention is the power of connecting one thought with another. It is an essentially inductive process, involving the formation of a habit.[39] This is what happens whenever attention is aroused by certain related aspects of experience. Someone burns a hand several times on a hot frying pan so that it demands attention. That person very soon develops a belief that the painful burning sensation will be linked to touching the frying pan under precisely these conditions. And that belief is a habit of action shaping one's future behavior with respect to frying pans. Now to the extent that attention can be controlled, this inductive process, too, can be controlled. Such control extends not only to the actual but also to the imagined elements of experience. For example, by attending in the imagination to the idea of certain actions performed in conjunction with certain circumstances, a disposition can be formed to execute those actions whenever the corresponding circumstances arise. This is how, on Peirce's account, the power of attention is utilized in the imagination to develop self-control. Notice that this process itself requires self-control—the ability to detach or remove oneself from the "forcible intrusion" into consciousness of various thoughts (what Peirce regarded as a form of "abstraction") in order to discern some meaningful pattern in experience.

Resolutions to act will be strengthened if accompanied by certain habitual feelings. These, too, can be exercised in the imagination, a strategy vividly exemplified by Ignatius of Loyola in the martial meditations sketched in his *Spiritual Exercises*. Emotions as well as actions can be inductively linked to specific types of events, objects, persons, or experiences. This is not so much a matter of programming oneself to have certain feelings under certain circumstances, no matter how artificial or inappropriate they may seem; rather, it is a matter of noticing "what may lie hidden in the icon," of attending to selected details and patterns in experience that may otherwise remain hidden beneath the threshold of consciousness.

How is it possible to develop an affection for the person that one had previously disliked? (An answer to this question would permit one at least to begin to make sense of the prescriptive talk in Christianity about love of enemies.) Whenever that person is encountered or imagined, one should identify and attend to specific attractive or praiseworthy features of his or her character. Paying attention to such positive features does not require suppressing or ignoring negative characteristics altogether. It does require noticing, by attending in a deliberate fashion, what one might have failed or neglected to notice before (an alternative might be to pursue the Buddhist strategy of becoming mindful of the various ways and the extent to which that person experiences suffering).[40] Observing these features will elicit certain feelings that can be transformed into a habitual interpretive response to that person, a gradual transformation of heart and mind. It takes practice, and that practice involves exercising self-control, but this is tantamount to a self-administered brainwashing only if that implies success in transforming oneself into the kind of person that one wanted to become in the first place.

The decision to become a particular sort of person is guided by selected models, values, or ideals, some of which may be religious in origin. This possibility underscores the potentially religious significance of developing the capacity for self-control. It also clearly suggests that developing self-control is not a project typically carried out by solitary individuals in isolation from communities of belief and interpretation. (A somewhat romantic image of the religious devotee or martial artist retreating into seclusion in order to pursue meditative disciplines can serve to reinforce such a distorted perspective. The perspective remains distorted even in cases where the image is accurate—for example, as in the case of Saint Antony of the Desert or the legendary Japanese swordsman Miyamoto Musashi.) Indeed, the self is socially constituted in multiple respects. Not only are many of the ideological resources available for such a project communal in origin, but many of the practices employed to develop self-control are rooted in the traditions of a community, organized and monitored by communal authorities. One of the central goals of religious or moral education is the training of individuals to be self-disciplined persons of a certain kind. Moreover, this goal is considered praiseworthy not simply or even primarily because self-controlled persons will display a certain form of behavior in private; their social behavior also will be affected, appropriate ideals becoming embodied in actual conduct, in habits of action and interaction, thus sustaining and enriching communal life.

Observing the social dimensions of religious discipline raises intriguing questions about the relationship between self-control and being controlled by another, or between self-control and the control of that which lies beyond the self. Consider first the hypothesis (presented early in this inquiry) that the greater the self-control a person possesses, the more power that person will be capable of exerting over others, while also being less vulnerable to the aggressive actions of others. This hypothesis is affirmed by the religious ideologies informing the practice of Asian martial disciplines like aikidō, taijiquan, and baguazhang. It is a hypothesis that resonates with the Confucian belief that an enormous power is embodied in the moral example of the virtuous, self-controlled individual; self-transformation is the most dramatic means for effecting significant and positive changes in the family, in society, and in the world.[41]

Peirce's own idealistic metaphysics also provides a home for this hypothesis. Without self-control, he conjectured, "the resolves and exercises of the inner world could not effect the real determinations and habits of the outer world." There is a very tangible sense, of course, in which one is directly and immediately capable of controlling things beyond oneself, like when one simply reaches out and opens the door to a room. But Peirce was especially interested in what he regarded as the more powerful but "indirect action of the inner world upon the outer through the operation of habits."[42] On Peirce's account, efficient causes should operate as the instruments of final causes; in other words, individual acts of volition have an enduring effect when they serve some greater purpose.

Peirce concluded that self-control is a kind of freedom. Yet he conceived of that freedom, in religious terms, as submission to the will of God. It is a tricky and a potentially dangerous business, both in this religious context and within the context formed by human relationships, closely to identify freedom with submission to the will of another. It might feel tremendously liberating to abdicate the responsibility for achieving self-discipline by allowing oneself to be controlled by another. But that can hardly be the type of perfect freedom that Peirce linked with the "service of Christ." In fact, it would seem to be the very opposite of genuine self-control.

One of the paradoxes of self-control, nevertheless, is exposed by this observation that it is possible to experience an authentic freedom by actually surrendering one's autonomy—by binding oneself to the will of another. This paradox is softened, once again, by shifting attention away from volition exercised over choices immediately available to a consideration of objectives that can only be achieved in the long run. If the development of self-control is a matter of gradual habit formation, then submission to the authority of some religious teacher or sage or deity might readily be conceived as a powerful method of self-transformation (despite the fact that it involves, most immediately, a necessary sacrifice of autonomy).

Of course, the judgment that acts of obedience would be likely to produce these desirable long-term effects is one requiring, in any given case, a certain power of discernment. It also presupposes an awareness or recognition of the value of developing a habit of detachment. Much of the literature on meditation and the martial arts is devoted to commentary on the importance of detachment, a disciplined rising above egoistic desires, impulses, and perspectives in order to achieve "a love of what is good for all on the whole." Obedience to a spiritual authority might be advocated for some of the same reasons that yielding to an aggressive opponent in combat can be strategically felicitous. Both are exercises in detachment. If painful at first, such detachment is potentially to be experienced as a freedom from the hegemony of certain desires. Self-control, in its most perfected form, is synonymous with this power of detachment. It is a removing of oneself from the distracting, potentially enslaving influence of specific impulses, a habitual readiness to pay attention to whatever is judged to matter most.

Peirce was certainly not a proponent of submission to authority as an effective method for fixing belief.[43] Yet he did advocate, in his only extended discussion of the abductive logic of meditation, or "musement," the practice of submitting in free and open attentiveness of heart and mind to the divine communication embedded in the universes of experience.[44] This "lively give and take of communion between self and self" is a free yet self-controlled form of playfulness; in a rather literal sense, for Peirce, it was a kind of falling in love.

There is a qualified sense in which both acts of contemplation and of love can require the surrender of control to another. Both also require careful attention to that other (the beloved, or the object of contemplation). And each has the potential to effect dramatic changes within the self. The condition of being in love is a binding of oneself to another that can, nevertheless and somewhat paradoxically, feel like perfect freedom. This can play itself out in a degenerate form when it involves the surrender to "temporary urgencies," a temporary feeling of liberation that results in enslavement. But it might also take the form of a rising above such urgencies in order to embrace an "extended view" of things, a love that endures in the long run precisely because it is freely given and self-controlled.

William James sought a moral equivalent of war in order to ensure the training of "societies to cohesiveness." And Charles Peirce's meditations on self-control clearly exposed its essence as a "love of what is good for all on the whole." Consistent with these perspectives, Josiah Royce articulated a "philosophy of loyalty" in the early decades of the twentieth century, once again emphasizing the social character and purpose of martial virtue.

Now Royce clearly conceived of loyalty as being more than merely martial in its significance. His account, both in *The Philosophy of Loyalty* and in his later work *The Problem of Christianity*, explored a wide range of applications for the term *loyalty*, including its meaning in a specifically religious (Christian) context. Yet it is interesting to observe that Royce was himself quite familiar with Nitobe's famous book on bushidō, and that he regarded the Japanese warrior's code as possessing a "wonderful spiritual power." Consider Royce's characterization of the samurai:

His whole early training involved a repression of private emotions, a control over his moods, a deliberate cheer and peace of mind, all of which he conceived to be a necessary part of his knightly equipment. Chinese sages, as well as Buddhistic traditions, influenced his views of the cultivation of this interior self-possession and serenity of soul. And yet he was also a man of the world, a warrior, an avenger of insults to his honor; and above all, he was loyal. His loyalty, in fact, consisted of all these personal and social virtues together.[45]

Equanimity and self-control were clearly aspects of the martial character that Royce admired. But his primary interest in the Japanese warrior tradition was a function of the degree to which it involved the cultivation of an intense loyalty.

Now loyalty was less a solitary virtue than a composite of virtues for Royce, their sum and perfection. He defined it as consisting in "the willing and practical and thoroughgoing devotion of a person to a cause."[46] This definition served as the stimulus for a philosophical inquiry that Royce pursued at considerable length. The details of that inquiry cannot be examined fully here, but a number of observations concerning Royce's definition of loyalty can be articulated in a few brief remarks.

In the first place, whatever its emotional content, loyalty was not something that Royce was inclined to reduce to a matter of feeling. It was essentially volitional on his account, an exercise of the will in producing "devotion . . . to a cause." That devotion was not something abstract but rather was a "practical" affair, to be visibly displayed in actual conduct. Despite his philosophical differences from Peirce, more especially from James, Royce was clearly a pragmatist in this regard. Finally, it was in this devotion to a cause that Royce perceived the social impulse to be most clearly manifested. In the service of a cause, individuals will surrender their own interests, sacrifice private concerns. Moreover, in their commitment to common causes, separate persons are bound to one another, forming cohesive communities of interest.

The sacrifice of private interests does not simply put an end to volition. Individuals are transformed by their loyalty so that their wills becomes unified in the blending of private and social concerns. For Royce, this was especially true of loyalty conceived as a martial virtue. The "war-spirit," he argued, "makes self-sacrifice seem to be self-expression, makes obedience to the country's call seem to be the proudest sort of display of one's own powers. Honor now means submission, and to obey means to have one's way. Power and service are at one. Conformity is no longer opposed to having one's own will."[47] Royce considered service to be a kind of power in the same way that Peirce regarded it potentially as a form of freedom. But Royce also recognized that freedoms can collide, that the power of separate loyalties can generate opposition. It was the possibility of just such a con-. flict that inspired his reflections on the highest form of loyalty as a loyalty to loyalty itself.

At first inspection, the phrase *loyalty to loyalty* seems to suggest the rendering absolute of loyalty as a virtue, so that the value of loyalty supersedes even the value of the cause to which one is devoted. There is an element of truth in this observation. The consequence of embracing this view, however, is just the opposite of endorsing a fanatical devotion—that is, one preserved beyond all reason and at any cost. Insofar as loyalty itself is preeminent, no dedication to a lesser cause will be sufficient motivation for a conflict that results in the destruction of persons, their differing causes and commitments. "If loyalty is a supreme good, the mutually destructive conflict of loyalties is a supreme evil. If loyalty is a good for all sorts and conditions of men, the war of man against man has been especially mischievous, not so much because it has hurt, maimed, impoverished, or slain men, as because it has so often robbed the defeated of their causes, of their opportunities to be loyal, and sometimes of their very spirit of loyalty."[48] This rendering absolute of loyalty as a value is a way of safeguarding against the potential destructiveness of a zealous devotion to specific causes; at the same time, it provides a criterion for the purpose of evaluating every form of devotion. "And so, a cause is good, not only for me but for mankind, in so far as it is essentially a *loyalty to loyalty,* that is, is an aid and a furtherance of loyalty in my fellows. It is an evil cause in so far as, despite the loyalty that it arouses in me, it is destructive of loyalty in the world of my fellows."[49]

Loyalty, quite obviously, was not a slavish form of submission for Royce, not something "blind and pathetic." Indeed, what Royce admired about the Japanese martial ideal was the fact that even "if it has discouraged strident self-assertion, it has not suppressed individual judgment."[50] Conscience is not expunged by, but rather perfected in, the loyal disposition. A rational person will be free to evaluate certain causes as evil and so to judge the loyalty to them as problematic. In Royce's view, many of the battles that have actually been fought in human history involved participants whose loyalty was problematic in just such a fashion.

Royce's higher "loyalty to loyalty" can justify a certain kind of pacifism, then, while nevertheless itself being imbued with a powerful martial spirit. Those persons devoted to the supreme cause of loyalty will feel compelled, even as Peirce had suggested, to engage in the "grimmest fight to put down the principle of self-seeking, and to make the principle of love triumphant." Now this way of putting the matter was by no means distinctively Peircean. Royce himself was inclined to identify loyalty in its most spiritually developed form as a kind of love. Already in his earlier work, Royce had portrayed the loyalty to loyalty as a love that moves a person to protect the freedom and commitments of other individuals. And in later discussion in *The Problem of Christianity*, Royce explicitly equated loyalty with the Christian love preached by Saint Paul in his letters. On this later account, a supreme loyalty is the work of charity and so of divine grace, not simply a devotion that individuals generate through volition, but a spirit working in the community, moving through persons and transforming them.[51]

At the same time, as the remarks above should have clearly indicated, loyalty *was* for Royce very much a matter of volition. This is one of the distinctive features of his account that closely links it to the perspectives of James and Peirce (as well as to certain subsequent philosophical discussions).[52] It is also one of the philosophical keys to understanding the relevance of the martial character to the spiritual life, and consequently the relationship between meditation and the martial arts.

Volition, attention, and love form an important trinity of

concepts for many of the spiritual writers and philosophers surveyed here. Attention is directed by the will (from James's point
of view, it is virtually synonymous with it). Moreover, one cannot claim to love that to which one never attends. In this fundamental sense, the quality of one's love is determined by the
quality of one's attention. Paying a certain kind of attention (as
in religious contemplation) can inspire love, strengthen it, and
sustain it. And one's decision to pay attention to this rather than
that constitutes the volitional essence of every act of love. Of
course, it is not always a simple matter of decision. Attention can
also be aroused by some stimulus, be "captured" by something
or someone, even in ways that violate a person's will or best intentions. That is how conflicts arise, making it appropriate to describe the business of attention in martial categories, explaining
also why it is very much a matter of self-control.

The pragmatists argued that persons are not perfectly isolated and autonomous egos moving about the world randomly
directing their attention here or there (like an individual wandering in a dark place shining a flashlight arbitrarily on this or
that object). The choosing to attend is not always executed on
the spot but often planned in advance, as individuals are formed
by their participation in communities, develop and share interests, and sometimes fall in love. Their commitments to these
loves and interests (recall firmitas in Duns Scotus) require the
development of certain habits of attention, a deliberate, self-
controlled process that Peirce took great pains to describe. Attention is important, then, not only in its implications for the
object of attention (the beloved person, the vital project, the political or social cause, etc.), but in its general significance for the
individual who directs and sustains it.

The consistent, disciplined practice of attention is a process
that Peirce analyzed in terms of the logic of induction. But once
habits have been effectively formed, they play a crucial role in
shaping a person's perceptions and interpretations (partially
determining what that person will now judge to be significant

and worthy of attention), a semiotic phenomenon the logical essence of which, for Peirce, was abductive.[53] Abduction can take on a playful, disinterested quality, as it does in the practice of musement. There, inductively formed beliefs and habits continue to shape semiosis, but not by rigidly determining interpretations of experience. Musement, at least initially, is a discipline of waiting, of listening, an attending-in-readiness to whatever appears. As such, abductive inquiry complements the logic of induction in the same way that the development of a certain habit of detachment was described earlier as both complementing and modifying the effects of particular skills and tendencies cultivated in martial exercises. Inductively, one establishes certain habits of attention. In musement, one playfully explores these dispositions, testing their limitations, softening their effects. This disciplined playfulness maintains attention as a living phenomenon. It prevents a person from continuing to experience someone or something in a manner completely defined by *habitus*. One's loyalty or love, one's commitment to any relationship, implies a readiness always to be surprised by what "may lie hidden in the icon," a contemplative attitude that assumes the most highly developed capacity for self-control.

The martial arts are disciplines of attention, importantly so, since the consequences of neglecting to pay proper attention in combat, of failing to perceive others correctly or interpret their behavior accurately, can be disastrous. Similarly, meditation in various religious traditions can be portrayed in martial images because the spiritual significance of paying proper attention is underscored in those traditions and the potential threats to attention are considered to be ubiquitous. This is perhaps the best way, in general terms, to understand the value of training in meditation and the martial arts for persons living in the twenty-first century. In a high-information environment, the potential candidates for attention, the possibilities of distraction and noise, are multiplied astronomically. This is not a merely bothersome, but otherwise benign, state of affairs. Not all instances of choosing are morally and spiritually neutral, as if they were all comparable to the situation of being overwhelmed by the large number of meal items on a diner menu: one may ponder which to choose, but then what is really at stake in the act of deciding? In contrast, how one chooses to direct one's attention can have life-or-death consequences, especially within the context of a war. In the information age, there is a tremendous competition to attract and fix the attention of individuals, thus also controlling their interests and desires for a whole variety of political and economic purposes. It is important to be able to resist this manipulation of attention and desire. Meditation is martial to the extent that it constitutes just such a discipline of resistance.[54]

Forces outside the self can struggle to capture an individual's attention, subsequently shaping that person's loyalties and desires. These "forces" can be embodied in specific individuals or groups with explicit and hostile motives; but they may also appear as a less-organized threat to the integrity of the self, a threat the nature of which is considerably more vague. Note that the effects of this struggle are experienced within the self, in the form of sadness, excitement, confusion, distraction, or violently conflicting impulses. For this reason, the battle waged against such forces will typically be waged on an interior battleground and a person's "self" will often be identified as the primary enemy. A variety of perspectives explored here—ranging from the Daoist view of the self as a "country" to Peirce's semiotic conception of the person as a continuous stream of self-interpreting symbols—suggest how this sort of identification might be rendered intelligible. It requires an appropriately complex but certainly not a schizophrenic view of the self to ground such intelligibility, an awareness, once again, of the link between microcosm and macrocosm or, in pragmatic terms, the degree to which the self, its habits and desires, are all socially constituted. Such talk will not seem fantastic or even highly metaphorical to anyone who has had the basic human experience that Saint Paul so vividly described, of doing what one would prefer not to do, a sense of bitter defeat that results when the will is split and set against itself.

One of the consequences of living in a high-information environment is that the self can become overwhelmed by noise and lapse into a state of spiritual numbness. This is a different kind of defeat from the one involving the capture of attention. It is less a matter of directing attention to the wrong object than an inability to exercise the will in directing attention at all. Here is another reason why the martial perspective offers both an accurate and effective means for understanding the spiritual life. The encounter with an enemy (indeed, the very idea of war), as William James suggested, will often wake a person up.

It may seem, perhaps, that there can be no "war" if there is no real conflict regarding a person's volition, if the attention is not actually threatened or conquered by some object of concern judged to be inappropriate. Yet to the extent that attention is considered a prerequisite for any kind of love, this state of sluggish inattentiveness will be perceived as bordering on spiritual death. Life is limited in duration, and the amount of attention that one has to spend is itself finite in quantity; it is a precious commodity, not to be spent foolishly, but of no value if never spent at all. Meditation on the fact of death is considered to be a spiritually felicitous practice, in Buddhism and in other religious traditions, precisely to the degree that it sparks attention and liberates the will from this otherwise anaesthetized condition.

The awakened self is typically a *grateful* self for all of the reasons described above. Readiness, attentive listening, and mindful waiting are all forms of active passivity, cultivated in martial/meditative practices through persistent training. Yet the more that one accomplishes in this regard, the greater one's awareness that the ultimate fruits of the spiritual life are not something that anyone can "accomplish." One can control certain aspects of the self, its will and desires, but this is a precondition for realizing the goal of the spiritual life and not that goal itself. William James, Zen masters, Muslim and Christian theologians have all carefully noted the gratuitous or gift-like character of spirituality's greatest satisfactions. They have recognized the lack of a simple cause-and-effect relationship between the rigorous exercises in which religious devotees engage and the levels of insight and peace that they subsequently might enjoy. That is not to suggest that the exercises are unimportant or irrelevant. But it does recommend a complicated account of what can be reasonably expected to result from such practices.

James, Peirce, and Royce were consistent with traditional religious perspectives in their philosophical insistence that the highest form of spiritual power is the power of love. James speculated about the extraordinary potential of the love of enemies; if perfectly cultivated it might effect a breach in the present "arrangement" of the universe, conceivably sufficient to "transform the world." Peirce perceived in love's "circular" movement a creative force guiding the process of cosmic evolution.[55] For Royce, the only cause worth fighting for was the cause of a supreme loyalty conceived as love, while the only true enemy was anyone or anything seeking to undermine loyalty-as-love.

To think about love as a kind of power with martial significance, as a "weapon" in the spiritual warrior's arsenal, is to wrestle with paradox, as well as to stretch the meaning of certain words used also to describe more mundane experiences. Still, a consensus has emerged here about how the power of such a love is manifested, in accounts ranging from the aikidō philosophy's appeal to alternative interpretations of human conflict to Charles Peirce's explication of the mechanics of self-control. In each case, love is described as a state of being detached from, thus unbound by, the exigencies of a particular situation. It does not represent a flight from the concrete struggles in which persons inevitably find themselves embroiled. Rather, love has a power to transfigure both self and situation by transcending their immediacy, potentially bringing them into harmony with a whole universe of selves and situations.

Postlude: On the Concept of Peace

There is no obvious contradiction between a philosophical commitment to nonviolence and the embracing of a martial perspective. The latter implies the recognition that there is some real evil to be resisted, something that genuinely threatens the self and its deepest interests. Nonviolence can be conceived as a possible strategy of resistance, a way of effectively countering evil rather than disastrously multiplying its effects. This is a dramatically simplified version of Mahatma Gandhi's point of view. It also represents the strategy embodied in many of the physical techniques of aikidō and the Chinese internal martial arts.

The fundamental presuppositions of a philosophy of nonviolence are not always clearly articulated or understood. They can imply a refusal to enhance the scope of violence. Yet they do not always entail an attempt to reduce or eliminate violence in all of its forms or manifestations. The effects of a nonviolent strategy of resistance, in the martial arts for example, can be spectacularly violent and destructive. It is not a matter of the person who resists contributing to this state of affairs in any direct fashion. The strategy is such that the violence is permitted rather than neutralized. To be crudely simplistic, consider what happens if one's back is against the wall while being confronted by an aggressor who rushes headlong to attack. One may respond in the most nonviolent manner, stepping aside to avoid the attack; at the same time, one does nothing to prevent the violent collision that occurs when the attacker meets the wall, with all of its destructive consequences.

It is a more difficult problem to determine whether or not pacifism is consistent with a martial spirituality. Nonviolence can be perceived as mode of resistance, the path to victory. But to what extent does talk about "resistance" or "victory" continue to make any sense from a pacifist's perspective? Phrases like *peaceful resistance* are sometimes employed to recommend a nonviolent course of action. This suggests that there is a considerable vagueness attached to some of the key terms being employed in the present analysis. Nevertheless, it is typically assumed that the concept of peace designates a state of affairs that is free of conflict, rather than a specific mode of engaging in any particular conflict.

The empirical fact of the matter is that proponents of a martial spirituality have frequently tended to identify themselves as pacifists, whatever possible philosophical contradictions may be involved in such a self-designation. Morihei Ueshiba regarded love as the true essence of budō and conceived of aikidō, fundamentally, as an "art of peace." Operative in the same Daoist ideology that shaped the Chinese martial arts was the idea of the Great Peace *(tai ping)*, an apocalyptic notion referring to a state of cosmic harmony that existed in primordial times and to which human beings were destined to return.[1] Appended to Lorenzo Scupoli's meditations on the spiritual combat is *A Treatise on Peace of Soul.* There he warned that it is precisely because the spiritual life is "nothing but a continual warfare" that "you must watch over your heart with a sedulous care that it may ever be at peace."[2]

For some persons, these examples will point to a way in which pacifism might be linked to a martial perspective, softening any apparent contradiction between the two. Peace is an ideal, having its primary reality *in futuro.* In actual fact, one must work—indeed, often fight—to secure this peaceful condition. There is a temporal gap, then, between the reality that inspires one's pacifism and that which necessitates one's martial point of view. Now this is a relatively straightforward explanation, but not one terribly helpful for understanding the literature surveyed here. Any war can be waged, ostensibly, in order to secure

the peace that ensues when the battle is over. In this rather trivial sense, every soldier and every weapon can be designated as a
"peacekeeper" or "peacemaker," and every act of war can be simultaneously conceived as an act of peace.

The examples cited above, as well as others that could be supplied, appear to require a different explanation. Peace *is* an ideal,
but also already something real for the spiritual devotee who attends to it and cultivates it. The more important gap revealed in
these examples is one between inner and outer realities. The spiritually disciplined person, it has repeatedly been argued, must
learn to maintain a peaceful state of equanimity even in the
midst of the most violent conflict. That was Krishna's advice to
Arjuna. It was the same advice that Scupoli was prescribing, as
well as Ueshiba and the Chinese martial sages.

This perspective does not advocate a retreat into the self at
the expense of allowing external conditions and relationships to
deteriorate into violence. Throughout this inquiry, a definite
causal connection has been established between one's interior
spiritual state and one's more general state of affairs. One works
directly on the body, heart, and mind in order eventually to
transform external circumstances. Moreover, one seeks to touch
the hearts and minds of others toward the end of creating enduring, peaceful relationships. On this view, the immediate
source of violence lies within the self.[3] (This is quite different
from making the claim that the ultimate causes of violence are
purely internal or that the mystery of evil is something that can
be reduced to an individual's psychic or spiritual impulses.) So,
too, the seeds of peace lie within the self, to be cultivated there
through spiritual discipline, but eventually bearing fruit in the
form of genuine community.

The idea of planting "seeds of peace" is not one typically encountered in the literature devoted to martial spirituality, although the metaphor has been commonly employed elsewhere,
especially in the writings of certain contemporary Buddhists.[4]
Ueshiba, interestingly enough, did insist on the connection at a

very basic level between budō and farming; it was his lifelong aspiration to unify the practice of aikidō with the practice of agriculture.[5] Equally intriguing is the observation that certain ancient Daoist texts designated those individuals who would survive in the coming kingdom of the Great Peace as "Seed People." From the perspective supplied by these texts, the meditative practice of "non-action" is also to be identified with the Great Peace, and the work of planting seeds of peace is identical to the ongoing task of qi gong.[6] Finally, in his 1893 essay on "evolutionary Love," Charles Peirce appealed to the image of "cherishing and tending . . . flowers in a garden" in order best to illustrate the discipline that love requires.[7] Elsewhere, Peirce had summoned his readers to take up the fight in order to make this same "principle of love triumphant." But here, too, the cosmic contest with evil and hatefulness supplied the necessary background for understanding the work of love. Indeed, genuine love always recognizes "germs of loveliness in the hateful," tending to them carefully, gradually warming them into life.

Like the growing of flowers in a garden, the practice of meditation is a gradual process of cultivation, requiring consistency in behavior, a loving attentiveness. The work can be arduous in either case; paradoxically, in neither case is the fruit of labor something that can always be measured precisely in proportion to the amount of energy invested. Many factors contribute to the growth of healthy plants—good soil, favorable weather conditions, and so forth. Similarly, the spiritual life is a work of cultivation that produces no guarantee of results. When the work bears fruit, both in the garden and in the life of the spirit, there is always reason and room for gratitude.

"Peace" is one way to label collectively the fruits of the spiritual life—inner peace as well as a relationship of harmony with everything that exists. Consider Paul's instruction in his letter to the Colossians: "Above all, clothe yourselves with love, which binds everything together in perfect harmony. And let the peace of Christ rule in your hearts, to which indeed you were called in the one body. And be thankful."[8] Compare this with his advice to the Ephesians, when he admonished them to put on the "whole armor of God." The latter offers guidance about how best to be prepared for combat with the evil one; the former is a teaching about how to live gratefully in Christ's peace. Yet the two instructions are essentially equivalent. Expected of the Christian in either case is a rigorous attention to spiritual discipline, the cultivation of virtue. What is made explicit in the passage from Colossians is the insight that love binds all of the virtues together "in perfect harmony."

This is a love that is stronger than death, a peace undisturbed by the challenge of death. "Making love" or "making peace" is never the work of a solitary individual. It always involves responding to or conspiring with forces that transcend the self. In the New Testament, peace is always something that Christ gives. This sort of peace cannot be manufactured in spiritual practice. But the conditions that preclude it can be gradually eroded through discipline, as conditions more felicitous for peace are continually built up.

Scupoli wrote about the human enslavement to desire as one such negative factor, rendering the self vulnerable to the tyranny of death.[9] As a mode of resistance, he counseled, "let us not consciously attach our wills to any one thing." Such an unfettered spirit will "leave the dead to bury their dead, forsaking the land of the lifeless for the land of the living." This is like the enlightened person described as one of the "companions of life" in the *Dao de jing.* He experiences the fullness of a peace that is inviolable, "for in him rhinoceroses can find no place to thrust their horn, . . . weapons no place to pierce. Why is this so? Because he has no place for death to enter."[10]

Notes

Introduction

1. Takuan Soho, *The Unfettered Mind,* trans. William Scott Wilson (New York: Kodansha International, 1986), p. 37.

2. Many scholars are convinced that Paul was not the author of the letter to the Ephesians; but on most accounts, the actual author would have been a disciple of Paul or a member of the Pauline school.

3. Saint Paul, Ephesians 6:13–17 (all biblical quotations taken from the New Revised Standard Version of the Bible).

4. Readers interested in the details of such a survey should consult Michael Maliszewski's *Spiritual Dimensions of the Martial Arts* (Rutland, Vt.: Tuttle, 1996).

5. One potential problem arises as a result of my portraying these various martial and meditative practices as disciplines of self-transformation, all designed to develop the practitioner's capacity for self-control. One must be careful in invoking some concept of the "self" that can be applied to Daoist, Hindu, Buddhist, and Christian texts alike. Of course, "self" is a vague notion, not only in my usage but notoriously so in virtually all philosophical discussions. I confess that this book presents no elaborate metaphysics of selfhood. But insofar as I draw upon a Peircean account of the self as a continuous stream of semiosis (in chapter 5), my admittedly vague perspective may actually be closer to some Buddhist accounts than to a traditional Hindu or Christian perspective. Moreover, some contemporary Buddhist thinkers (like Thich Nhat Hanh) have argued that it is as dangerous to speak in absolute terms about "no-self" as it is to affirm the existence of the self as substantial. And even Buddhists who vigorously defend the doctrine of no-self *(anatman)* embrace disciplines of "self-control"; this does not commit them, metaphysically speaking, to a belief in real essences.

6. Many of John Stevens's writings and translations document the religious background of aikidō; see, for example, his *The Essence of Aikido: Spiritual Teachings of Morihei Ueshiba* (Tokyo: Kodansha International, 1993). Consider also William Gleason's *The Spiritual Foundations of Aikido* (Rochester, Vt.: Destiny Books, 1995).

7. I have in general employed the pinyin system for expressing Chinese terms and names (e.g., taijiquan, baguazhang, qi, Laozi), not what to some readers may be the more familiar Wade-Giles expressions (tai chi chuan, pa kua chang, ch'i, Lao Tzu). In quotations and in the notes, however, I use the spelling that appears in my English sources.

1. The Way of Spiritual Harmony

1. Morihei Ueshiba, *The Art of Peace: Teachings of the Founder of Aikido*, comp. and trans. John Stevens (Boston, Mass.: Shambhala, 1992), p. 8.

2. Quoted in John Stevens's popular biography of Ueshiba, *Abundant Peace: The Biography of Morihei Ueshiba* (Boston, Mass.: Shambhala, 1987), p. 112. Stevens has translated the majority of Ueshiba's writings now available in English. His intention has been to make Ueshiba's teachings more broadly accessible, rather than to provide a critical, scholarly account. I draw extensively on Stevens's work, but my primary concern here is with the philosophy of aikidō as articulated by Ueshiba and others, not in details of Ueshiba's life.

3. Ueshiba, *Art of Peace*, p. 99.

4. Morihei Ueshiba, *Budo*, trans. John Stevens (Tokyo: Kodansha International, 1991), p. 31.

5. Ueshiba, *Art of Peace*, pp. 34–35.

6. Ibid., p. 99.

7. Ibid., p. 43.

8. Ueshiba, *Budo*, p. 32.

9. Stevens, *Essence of Aikido*, p. 29. Attentive to the Westerners in his audience and partially influenced by Western theism (as were many others in Ōmoto-kyō), Ueshiba appears to have engaged in a certain amount of talk about the divine reality as a personal God. But it should be noted that the idea of *kami* as divine forces or spirits in traditional Shintō cannot simply be conflated with the concept of God in classical Western monotheism. Not only does it appear that Ueshiba was creatively appropriating and adapting elements of that tradition, but also his intended meanings for certain terms may differ from the ones most readily applied to their English translations by some readers. For a brief discussion of the Shinto kami concept, see *The Encyclopedia of Religion* (New York: Macmillan, 1987), volume 8; s.v., *"Kami,"* by Ueda Kenji.

10. Stevens, *Essence of Aikido*, p. 97 ff.

11. Kisshomaru Ueshiba, *The Spirit of Aikido* (Tokyo: Kodansha International, 1987), p. 53.

12. The Gospel narratives typically portray the resurrected Jesus as

breathing on his disciples as he offers them his peace and imparts the Holy Spirit; e.g., John 20:19–23.

13. Quoted by Mitsugi Saotome in *Aikido and the Harmony of Nature* (Boston, Mass.: Shambhala, 1993), p. 154.

14. For a detailed discussion of Ueshiba's practice of the recitation of the kotodama, see Gleason, *Spiritual Foundations of Aikido,* chapter 4; and John Stevens, *The Secrets of Aikido* (Boston, Mass.: Shambhala, 1995), pp. 15–26.

15. I offer a brief philosophical account of the role played by redundancy in certain spiritual practices in "Ritual, Redundancy, and the Religious Imagination," chapter 4 of *Boredom and the Religious Imagination* (Charlottesville: University Press of Virginia, 1999), pp. 105–35.

16. Stevens, *Essence of Aikido,* pp. 25–26.

17. Ibid., p. 99. For a brief but interesting discussion of the importance of gratitude as an element in the spirituality of the Japanese new religions, see Helen Hardacre, *Kurozumikyo and the New Religions of Japan* (Princeton, N.J.: Princeton University Press, 1986), pp. 23–26.

18. Stevens, *Secrets of Aikido,* pp. 120–21.

19. The analysis of self-control as an act of volition primarily directed toward the future is developed within the context of my discussion of some of Peirce's ideas in chapter 5.

20. Yuasa Yasuo offered a fascinating philosophical and psychological account of how the martial arts and similar exercises represent attempts to transform the mind (in both its conscious and unconscious aspects) by rigorously training the body; see *The Body, Self-Cultivation and Ki-Energy,* trans. Shigenori Nagatomo and Monte S. Hull (Albany: State University of New York Press, 1993).

21. The implications of this claim are more clearly articulated in chapter 5, where these martial practices are interpreted through the lens supplied by the pragmatism of Peirce, Royce, and James.

22. For additional comments on the concept of detachment, see "The Logic of Indifference" in my *Boredom and the Religious Imagination,* pp. 72–104.

23. Ueshiba, *Art of Peace,* pp. 16–17.

24. Ibid., p. 67.

25. Hardacre detects a certain Neo-Confucianist influence on the Japanese new religions, shaping their perspective on self-cultivation and self-effort; see *Kurozumikyo and the New Religions of Japan,* pp. 14–21.

2. Daoist Moving Meditation

1. See Cheng Man-Ch'ing, *Cheng Man-Ch'ing's Advanced T'ai-Chi Form Instructions,* comp. and trans. Douglas Wile (Brooklyn, N.Y.: Sweet Ch'i

Press, 1985), pp. 12–13. For another account that links the use of the designation "external" to the Buddhist influence on such martial arts, consider Donn F. Draeger and Robert W. Smith, *Asian Fighting Arts* (Tokyo:
Kodansha International, 1973), p. 17. My purpose here is not to endorse
the claim that the internal martial arts have never been influenced by Buddhism, but rather to suggest that the historical origins of the internal/
external distinction may be linked to the desire to argue for such a claim.
In *Lost Tai-Chi Classics,* Wile explicates that desire in terms of the Chinese
need symbolically to affirm their identity in resistance to the hegemony of
"outsiders," its particular manifestation in the nineteenth century being "a
psychological defense against Western cultural imperialism"; see Wile, *Lost
Tai-Chi Classics from the Late Ch'ing Dynasty* (Albany: State University of
New York Press, 1996), esp. pp. 25–26.

2. Sun Lu Tang, *Xing Yi Quan Xue: The Study of Form-Mind Boxing,* trans.
Albert Liu, ed. Dan Miller (Burbank, Calif.: Unique Publications, 2000). In
the introduction to this work, a biographical sketch of Sun Lutang documents his training in and blending of these three martial arts; see pp. 2–41.

3. See "Prevention and Cure of Sickness," in Da Liu, *T'ai Chi Ch'uan
and Meditation* (New York: Schocken Books, 1986), chapter 13. For a comprehensive treatment of the art of taijiquan that offers an extended consideration of its significance for the promotion of health and longevity, see
the important study by Catherine Despeux, *Taiji Quan, art martial, technique de longue vie* (Paris: Guy Tredaniel, 1985).

4. From the translation of the taiji classics in Tsung-Hwa Jou, *The Tao
of Tai-Chi Chuan,* ed. Shoshana Shapiro (Warwick, N.Y.: Tai Chi Foundation, 1985), p. 181.

5. Wile, *Lost Tai-Chi Classics from the Late Ch'ing Dynasty,* p. 55.

6. Ibid., p. 51.

7. *Lao-Tzu: Te-Tao Ching,* trans. Robert G. Henricks (New York: Modern
Library, 1993), chapter 10, p. 64.

8. Da Liu, *T'ai Chi Ch'uan and Meditation;* for a mapping of the meridian system with a discussion of its significance for Daoist meditation, see
chapter 3, "Fundamentals of Chinese Physiology," pp. 34–48.

9. Matthew 18:3–4.

10. *Lao Tsu: Tao Te Ching,* trans. Gia-Fu Feng and Jane English (New
York: Vintage, 1997), chapter 55.

11. Ibid., chapter 76.

12. Tsung-Hwa Jou, *Tao of Tai-Chi Chuan,* pp. 182–83.

13. Zheng Manqing (Ch'eng Man-Ch'ing) recalled how, in his training, his teacher Yang Ch'eng-fu repeatedly urged him to "Relax!": *Cheng
Man-Ch'ing's Advanced T'ai-Chi Form Instructions,* pp. 10–11. Of course, it is

notoriously difficult to relax on command or by a simple act of volition. Zheng reported that his breakthrough occurred after he dreamed that both his arms were broken; awakening, he felt totally relaxed like a "Raggedy Ann doll." My own teacher has recommended the experiment of trying to do the taiji form as if paralyzed from the waist up, allowing all movement of the upper body and arms to be dictated by the shifting of weight and turning of the waist.

14. Henricks explicitly associates the relevant line in chapter 10 with "Taoist longevity techniques"; see p. xxxi of his introduction to *Lao-Tzu: Te-Tao Ching*. For a discussion of Daoist techniques of "prenatal" or "embryonic" breathing, see Da Liu, "The Tao of Breathing," in *T'ai Chi Ch'uan and Meditation*, chapter 4, esp. pp. 50–51; see also Kristofer Schipper's *The Taoist Body*, trans. Karen C. Duval (Berkeley: University of California Press, 1993), section on "The Return," pp. 155–59. These techniques, combining regulated breathing with elaborate visualizations, are part of the complex methodology of a Daoist "internal alchemy" designed to produce powerful transformations within the body with the goal of achieving long life, potentially, immortality.

15. *Chuang Tzu: Basic Writings*, trans. Burton Watson (New York: Columbia University Press, 1996), p. 54.

16. Isabelle Robinet, *Taoist Meditation: The Mao-Shin Tradition of Great Purity*, trans. Julian F. Pas and Norman J. Girardot (Albany: State University of New York Press, 1993), p. 84.

17. Cheng Man-ch'ing and Robert W. Smith, *T'ai-Chi: The "Supreme Ultimate" Exercise for Health, Sport, and Self Defense* (Rutland, Vt.: Tuttle, 1990), p. 2.

18. For a brief philosophical treatment of this topic, see the postlude to my *Boredom and the Religious Imagination*, "On Waiting."

19. Watson, trans., *Chuang Tzu: Basic Writings*, pp. 86–87.

20. Cheng Man-Ch'ing, *Cheng Man-Ch'ing's Advanced T'ai-Chi Form Instructions*, pp. 107, 112–13.

21. Traditional stories link Dong Haichuan to "Complete Reality" or "Perfect Truth" *(Chuan Chen)* Daoism, and more particularly to the Dragon Gate *(Lung Men)* sect; see John Bracy and Liu Xing-Han, *Ba Gua: Hidden Knowledge in the Taoist Internal Martial Art* (Berkeley: North Atlantic Books, 1998), p. 2; see also Dan Miller, "The Circle Walk Practice of Ba Gua Zhang," in *Pa Kua Chang Journal* 4, no. 6 (1994): 4. This form of Daoism has incorporated significant elements of Chan Buddhism, as well as of Confucianism, but its primary agenda is the refining of energies and elements within the self as defined by the principles of Daoist internal alchemy. For a fascinating narrative portrayal of Lung Men spiritual prac-

tices, see Chen Kaiguo and Zheng Shunchao, *Opening the Dragon Gate: The Making of a Modern Taoist Wizard*, trans. Thomas Cleary (Boston, Mass.: Tuttle, 1998). The book describes a young devotee's engaging in "equilibrium exercises," combining "harmonic physical movements with strictly regulated breathing patterns." Some of the exercises involved walking in a "horse step" beneath a net strung between trees at a low height, the head continuously touching the net so that the devotee's legs were crouching "but his upper body erect." He eventually became so skillful, his legs so powerful, that he could move about in this low posture at high speeds carrying a bowl of water on his head while "keeping the surface of the water level as a mirror." In some forms, this walking exercise actually included intense concentration on imagined "eight trigram mental balls," with the practitioner moving swiftly from one to the next, "his upper body remaining erect and balanced throughout, blending different hand positions and different breathing patterns into an infinitely varied flux" (pp. 41–49).

22. Schipper, *Taoist Body*, p. 222, note 2.

23. From Robert W. Smith and Allen Pittman, *Pa-Kua: Eight-Trigram Boxing* (Rutland, Vt.: Tuttle, 1989), p. 15.

24. John Bracy and Liu Xing-Han, *Ba Gua*, p. xix.

25. Schipper has an illuminating discussion of the Daoist perspective on the body as "country" or "landscape " in *Taoist Body*; see esp. chapters 6 and 8.

26. Richard Wilhelm, *The I Ching, or Book of Changes*, translated from the German by Cary F. Branes (Princeton, N.J.: Princeton University Press, 1967), p. 295.

27. Sun Lutang, *Bagua Quan Xue: A Study of Eight Trigrams Boxing*, trans. Joseph Crandall and Helin Dong (Pinole, Calif., n.p., 1995), p. vii.

28. Ibid., p. 63.

29. Ibid., p. 64.

30. In a fascinating collection of essays, Sophia Delza, a distinguished instructor of the Wu style, emphatically rejected the characterization of taijiquan as a form of "moving meditation"; see Delza, *The T'ai-Chi Ch'uan Experience*, ed. Robert C. Neville (Albany: State University of New York Press, pp. 235–36.

31. See Robinet, *Taoist Meditation*, pp. 30–31, and Schipper, *Taoist Body*, p. 137.

32. It is interesting to speculate about a possible relationship between the Daoist circle-walking meditation that may have influenced baguazhang and the ancient Daoist "march on the stars," a ritual dance that traced the circular paths of heavenly bodies while moving vital energy

within the body in corresponding microcosmic patterns; see brief discussion in Robinet, *Taoist Meditation*, pp. 221–25.

3. Yoga/Zen/Jihad

1. For an account of some historically prominent perspectives on the Bhagavad Gita, consult Arvind Sharma's *The Hindu Gita: Ancient and Classical Interpretations of the Bhagavadgita* (La Salle, Ill.: Open Court, 1986). Robert Minor has edited a volume of essays on some modern readings of the poem: *Modern Indian Interpreters of the Bhagavadgita* (Albany: State University of New York Press, 1986).

2. *The Bhagavadgita*, trans. with commentary by R. C. Zaehner (Oxford: Oxford University Press, 1989), chapter 2, verses 17–25, p. 49.

3. Ibid., chapter 2, verses 47–48, p. 51.

4. Ibid., chapter 2, verses 50–53, pp. 51–52.

5. Ibid., see Zaehner's commentary on p. 143.

6. *Yoga Philosophy of Patanjali*, with commentary by Swami Hariharananda Aranya, trans. P. N. Mukerji (Albany: State University of New York Press, 1983), book 1, sutra 2, pp. 6–11.

7. Ibid., book 2, sutra 29, p. 207.

8. Jean Varenne, *Yoga and the Hindu Tradition*, trans. Derek Coltman (Chicago, Ill.: University of Chicago Press, 1976), p. 28.

9. Mircea Eliade, *Yoga: Immortality and Freedom*, trans. Willard R. Trask (Princeton, N.J.: Princeton University Press, 1969), pp. 332–33 and note 115.

10. *Bhagavadgita*, Zaehner, trans., chapter 5, verses 27–28, p. 64.

11. Ibid., chapter 18, verses 65–66, p. 108.

12. Ibid., chapter 3, verses 37–41 and 43, pp. 56–57. Compare these verses with Krishna's discourse in chapter 6, verses 1–32, where he describes the self, if not properly self-controlled, as its own chief enemy. On the other hand, "the higher self of the self-subdued" is that of one who is able to regard "in a selfsame way friends, comrades, enemies, those indifferent, neutrals, men who are hateful and those who are his kin" (verse 9). For Krishna, such a yogin is one "who standing firm on unity communes-in-love with Me as abiding in all beings, in whatever state he be, that athlete of the spirit abides in Me" (verse 31).

13. Consult Sharma's important essay "Hinduism," in *Our Religions*, ed. Arvind Sharma (San Francisco, Calif.: HarperCollins, 1993), esp. the sections on "Militant Hinduism," pp. 18–20, and "Modern Hinduism and the *Bhagavadgita*," p. 33.

14. *The Moral and Political Writings of Mahatma Gandhi*, ed. Raghavan

Iyer (Oxford: Oxford University Press, 1986), "The *Gita* and Non-Violence," pp. 77–83.

15. Trevor Leggett provides a sampling of classical literature relating Zen Buddhism to the martial arts in his commentary in *Zen and the Ways*, Leggett, trans. (Rutland, Vt.: Tuttle, 1987). See also Daisetz T. Suzuki's essays on "Zen and the Samurai" and "Zen and Swordsmanship" in *Zen and Japanese Culture* (Princeton, N.J.: Princeton University Press, 1970), chapters 3, 4, and 5; and the philosopher Eugen Herrigel's widely read meditations in *Zen in the Art of Archery* (New York: Vintage, 1989).

16. This caricature of religion as consisting of acts performed by "individual men in their solitude" appears in William James's comments at the beginning of *The Varieties of Religious Experience* (New York: Penguin, 1985), p. 31. But James's own account of religion was too rich and lively to be confined within the boundaries established by such a definition (see my discussion of James in chapter 5).

17. The significance of loyalty for martial spirituality is a topic introduced here but further developed later in connection with the philosophy of Josiah Royce. Here I want to emphasize that the code of the samurai represents an ideal, a prescribed ethic, not a description of the actual values and behavior of historical individuals. The evidence suggests that many Japanese samurai were ruthlessly self-interested, anything but loyal in this ideal sense. For a vivid portrait of the samurai, their motivations and conflicts, see Mary Elizabeth Berry, *The Culture of Civil War in Kyoto* (Berkeley: University of California Press, 1997). Consider, also, Winston King's discussion in *Zen and the Way of the Sword: Arming the Samurai Psyche* (New York: Oxford University Press, 1993).

18. For a clear and perceptive philosophical analysis of mushin, with insightful reference both to the Chinese prehistory of that notion and to parallel notions in Western thought, consult Thomas P. Kasulis, *Zen Action/Zen Person* (Honolulu: University Press of Hawaii, 1981), esp. chapters 3 and 4.

19. The image of mushin as an "immensity of space, blue like the bright sky" appears in Leggett, *Zen and the Ways*, p. 22.

20. Ibid., p. 23.

21. Soho, *Unfettered Mind*, p. 33.

22. Ibid., p. 35.

23. Shunryu Suzuki, *Zen Mind, Beginner's Mind* (New York: Weatherhill, 1970), p. 115.

24. For philosophical perspectives on the relationship between playfulness and detachment, see Raposa, *Boredom and the Religious Imagination*, pp. 88–104.

25. Legget, *Zen and the Ways*, pp. 136–37.

26. Suzuki, *Zen Mind, Beginner's Mind*, p. 21.

27. Ibid., p. 31.

28. Soho, *Unfettered Mind*, p. 87.

29. Ibid., p. 60.

30. *The Zen Master Hakuin: Selected Writings*, trans. Philip B. Yampolsky (New York: Columbia University Press, 1971), p. 219.

31. Soho, *Unfettered Mind*, p. 80.

32. Inazo Nitobe, *Bushido: The Soul of Japan* (Boston, Mass.: Tuttle, 1969), pp. 12–16. My interest in Nitobe on bushidō is largely a function of the use that Royce makes of this text in his own philosophizing. I recognize that Nitobe's account was itself shaped by a variety of ideological factors, that it may have embodied a rhetoric designed to justify Japanese militarism and to conceal a "totalitarian state ethics." But whatever its motivations, it draws on authentic resources from the Japanese spiritual traditions. For a nuanced discussion, see Steven Odin, *The Social Self in Zen and American Pragmatism* (Albany: State University of New York Press, 1996), esp. p. 42 ff.

33. Ibid., p. 92.

34. Rudolph Peters, *Jihad in Classical and Modern Islam* (Princeton, N.J.: Markus Wiener, 1996), pp. 1, 115–19.

35. *The Koran*, trans. N. J. Dawood (New York: Penguin Books, 1974), p. 313, chapter 16: 125.

36. Peters, *Jihad*, p. 116.

37. Gerhard Bowering, *The Mystical Vision of Existence in Classical Islam* (Berlin: Walter de Gruyter, 1980), p. 258.

38. See William C. Chittick's translation *The Sufi Path of Love: The Spiritual Teachings of Rumi* (Albany: State University of New York Press, 1983), p. 154. Consider, also, the following similar exhortations in Rumi: "The time for the Greater Holy War has come! Arise, oh Sufi! Enter the battle! Cut the throat of sensuality with hunger! Fret not over stew! The dervish gives away his body and spirit: This is the principle of every generous act. Place them in the fire, for fire is an alchemy that transforms the unripe" (p. 155); "So behead your selfhood, oh warrior! Become selfless and annihilated, like a dervish! When you have become selfless, you are secure in whatever you do: *Thou didst not throw when thou threwest, but God threw*" (p. 188; emphasis in the original).

39. Dawood, trans., *The Koran*, p. 52, chapter 79.

40. Refer to Annemarie Schimmel's review of images for portraying the control of the nafs in *Mystical Dimensions of Islam* (Chapel Hill: University of North Carolina Press, 1975). pp. 112–13.

41. For explication of the concept of dhikr, consult useful discussions by Bowering in *Mystical Vision of Existence*, pp. 201–7, and Schimmel in *Mystical Dimensions of Islam*, pp. 167–78.

42. Dawood, trans., *The Koran*, p. 145, 13:28.

43. Ibid., p. 348, 2:152. On gratitude as a fundamental religious attitude in Islam, see Schimmel, *Mystical Dimensions of Islam*, pp. 125–26, and Kenneth Cragg, *The House of Islam* (Belmont, Calif.: Dickenson, 1969), p. 61.

44. For analysis of dhikr as breathing meditation, see Frederick M. Denny, *An Introduction to Islam* (New York: Macmillan, 1985), pp. 286–87, and Schimmel, *Mystical Dimensions of Islam*, pp. 173–74.

45. Bowering, *Mystical Vision of Existence*, p. 243.

46. Titus Burckhardt, *An Introduction to Sufism: The Mystical Dimension of Islam*, trans. D. M. Matheson (Wellingborough, England: Aquarian Press, 1990), pp. 103–4. For an extended treatment (pictures and text) of the dance of the dervishes, see Ira Friedlander, *The Whirling Dervishes* (New York: Macmillan, 1975).

47. Chittick, *Sufi Path of Love*, pp. 327–28.

48. On faqr, see Schimmel, *Mystical Dimensions of Islam*, pp. 120–24.

49. Chittick, *Sufi Path of Love*, p. 155.

4. The Spiritual Combat

1. Matthew 10:34–36.

2. Matthew 26:52.

3. Luke 6:27–29.

4. R. C. Zaehner, *The Dawn and Twilight of Zoroastrianism* (London: Weidenfeld & Nicolson, 1961); a succinct "summary of the doctrine" is at pp. 60–61.

5. Ibid., pp. 20–21, 51–52, 57–58; see also J. Duchesne-Guillemin (Oxford, England: Clarendon, 1958), esp. the final chapter, "Iran, Israel, Gnosticism." Crucial for understanding this Zoroastrian influence on Judaism is the "Manual of Discipline" (sometimes identified as "The Community Rule"), one of the Dead Sea documents from Qumran. It portrays the world created by God as an arena of conflict between spirits of good and evil, between the "prince of light" and the "angel of darkness"; see *The Dead Sea Scrolls in English*, ed. Geza Vermes (London: Penguin Books, 1987), pp. 61–80, esp. pp. 64–65.

6. 1 Thessalonians 5:16–18. This exhortation, addressed to the "children of light and children of day," is part of an instruction that includes familiar martial imagery: "But since we belong to the day, let us be sober, and put on the breastplate of faith and love, and for a helmet the hope of salvation" (verse 8).

7. The classical portrayal of the monk's struggle with the midday demon appears at the beginning John Cassian's analysis "The Spirit of Acedia," written early in the fifth century; see John Cassian, *The Institutes*, trans. Boniface Ramsey, O.P. (New York: Newman Press, 2000), pp. 219–21; see also Reinhard Kuhn, *The Demon of Noontide: Ennui in Western Literature* (Princeton, N.J.: Princeton University Press, 1976), chapter 2, pp. 39–64.

8. Athanasius, *The Life of Antony and the Letter to Marcellinus*, trans. Robert C. Gregg (New York: Paulist Press, 1980), p. 42.

9. Ibid., p. 47 (italic in the original).

10. Ibid., p. 39. On Athanasius's concept of theopoiesis and its relevance to the Arian controversy, consult William A. Clebsch's preface, ibid., pp. xiii–xxi.

11. Since the purpose of this account is primarily philosophical, these brief remarks do not even begin to suggest the prominent role played by martial imagery in early Christian spirituality. For greater historical detail, see Adolf Harnack, *Militia Christi: The Christian Religion and the Military in the First Three Centuries*, trans. David McInnes Gracie (Philadelphia: Fortress Press, 1981), chapter 1. This useful essay is problematic only for the dubious assumption on Harnack's part that a martial symbolism applied to the spiritual life inevitably results in a "warlike mood" infecting Christianity and threatening the "norm of gentleness and peace"; see p. 32.

12. Thomas Aquinas, *Summa Theologica*, part 3, question 72, article 4 (italic in the original).

13. Ibid., reply to objection 3 (italic in the original).

14. Ibid.; see the treatise on fortitude in the second part of part 2, questions 123–40 (see esp. the early questions emphasizing the soldier's and martyr's courage in facing death, and question 136 on patience).

15. The collection of Scotus's writings most relevant to this discussion of martial spirituality is that contained in *Duns Scotus on the Will and Morality*, trans. Allan B. Wolter, O.F.M., with his invaluable commentary (Washington, D.C.: Catholic University of America Press, 1986); see esp. p. 179 ff, "The Will and Its Inclinations."

16. This experience of conversion and the degree to which it was shaped by Ignatius's self-image as a warrior has been explored by W. W. Meissner, S.J., in his brilliant biography *Ignatius of Loyola: The Psychology of a Saint* (New Haven, Conn.: Yale University Press, 1992, esp. pp. 18–65.

17. Ignatius of Loyola, *The Spiritual Exercises of St. Ignatius*, trans. Louis J. Puhl, S.J. (Chicago, Ill.: Loyola University Press, 1951), p. 44.

18. Ibid., p. 5.

19. Ibid., p. 142.

20. Ibid., p. 145.

21. Ibid., p. 144.

22. Ibid., p. 75; see also the "First Principle and Foundation," p. 12, as well as the culminating "Contemplation to Obtain the Love of God," pp. 101–3.

23. Ibid., pp. 60–63.

24. Ibid., pp. 107–11. For an insightful commentary, not only on these specific methods but on the entire strategy of the exercises, see Alexandre Brou, S.J., *Ignatian Methods of Prayer*, trans. William J. Young, S.J. (Milwaukee: Bruce, 1949).

25. Ibid., pp. 36, 107.

26. Ibid., pp. 157–61.

27. Dom Lorenzo Scupoli, *The Spiritual Combat, and a Treatise on Peace of Soul*, trans. William Lester and Robert Mohan (Rockford, Ill.: Tan Books, 1990), p. 186.

28. Ibid., p. 33.

29. Ibid., p. 7.

30. Ibid., p. 9.

31. Ibid., p. 14.

32. Ibid., p. 22.

33. Ibid., p. 23. With discipline, it is possible to use the senses (much as Ignatius had suggested) in a manner that is spiritually edifying. All beautiful things—animals, plants, other persons—become signs radiant with divine glory; see pp. 65–68.

34. Ibid., pp. 45, 46.

35. Ibid., p. 81.

36. Ibid., p. 131.

37. Ibid., p. 166.

38. Gregory Palamas, *The Triads*, ed. John Meyendorff, trans. Nicholas Gendle (New York: Paulist Press, 1983), p. 46.

39. Ibid., pp. 41–42.

40. Jonathan Edwards, *A Treatise Concerning Religious Affections*, ed. John E. Smith (New Haven, Conn.: Yale University Press, 1959). For a brief discussion of Edwards's theosemiotic, see my "Jonathan Edwards' Twelfth Sign," *International Philosophical Quarterly* 33 (June 1993): pp. 153–62.

41. Adolphe Tanquerey, *The Spiritual Life: A Treatise on Ascetical and Mystical Theology*, trans. Herman Branderis (Tournai, Belgium: Society of St. John the Evangelist, Desclee, 1930), esp. pp. 101–19.

42. For a powerful example of the sort of spirituality that best complements the perspective of liberation theology, consult Gustavo Gutier-

rez, *We Drink from Our Own Wells* (Maryknoll, N.Y.: Orbis Books, 1984), esp. p. 54 ff.

5. *Toward a Moral Equivalent of War*

1. William James, "The Moral Equivalent of War," in *Essays on Faith and Morals,* ed. Ralph Barton Perry (Cleveland, Ohio: Meridian Books, 1962). These items are culled from lists that appear In James's essay, pp. 319 and 323.

2. Ibid., p. 321.

3. Ibid., p. 325.

4. Ibid., p. 326.

5. Ibid., p. 325.

6. Ibid., p. 328.

7. James, "The Energies of Men," in *Essays on Faith and Morals,* p. 221.

8. Ibid., p. 229.

9. Ibid., p. 232.

10. William James, *The Varieties of Religious Experience* (New York: Penguin Books, 1982), p. 367.

11. Ibid., p. 362.

12. Ibid., pp. 166–67.

13. Ibid., p. 319.

14. Ibid., see pp. 367–68.

15. Ibid., pp. 45–46.

16. On the relation between volition and attention in James's philosophical psychology, see Richard Gale's *The Divided Self of William James* (Cambridge: Cambridge University Press, 1999), esp. p. 51.

17. James, *Varieties of Religious Experience,* pp. 283–84.

18. Ibid., p. 151.

19. For a superbly written narrative that measures the impact of the Civil War on James, Peirce, and a whole generation of American intellectuals, consider Louis Menand's account in *The Metaphysical Club* (New York: Farrar, Straus & Giroux, 2001).

20. Charles S. Peirce, *Collected Papers of Charles Sanders Peirce,* ed. C. Hartshorne, P. Weiss, and A. Burks (Cambridge: Harvard University Press, 1935, 1958), 6:448 (vol. 6, para. 448).

21. I review some of the plot of that story in *Peirce's Philosophy of Religion* (Bloomington: Indiana University Press, 1989); see esp. chapter 3, "Evolutionary Love," pp. 63–92.

22. The bulk of the analysis that follows is a slightly revised and expanded version of my article "Self Control," *American Journal of Theology & Philosophy* 21 (September 2000): 256–68.

23. Peirce, *Collected Papers*, 5:339, note 1. See also 5:402, note 3.

24. See Joseph Brent's account and commentary in *Charles Sanders Peirce: A Life* (Bloomington: Indiana University Press, 1993), esp. pp. 13–15.

25. Charles S. Peirce, *Semeiotic and Significs: The Correspondence between Charles S. Peirce and Victoria Lady Welby*, ed. Charles S. Hardwick (Bloomington: Indiana University Press, 1977). See Peirce's letter to Lady Welby dated March 14, 1909, esp. the passages on pages 112 and 114.

26. Peirce, *Collected Papers*, 8:320.

27. Ibid., 4:611.

28. Ibid., 5:339, note 1.

29. Ibid., 5:418.

30. Ibid., 5:402, note 3.

31. Ibid., 5:310–17 and 6:270.

32. This perspective on religious experience is articulated both in my commentary on Peirce's "Neglected Argument" in chapter 5 of *Peirce's Philosophy of Religion* and in the Peircean meditations on religious boredom and insight that form the subtance of chapters 4 and 5 in my *Boredom and the Religious Imagination*.

33. Peter Van Ness has analyzed spiritual discipline as both a method of habit formation and a means of resisting the attempt made by others to control us by controlling our habits of perception and action; see Van Ness, *Spirituality, Diversion, and Decadence: The Contemporary Predicament* (Albany: State University of New York Press, 1992). While Van Ness does not explicitly make the connection, his analysis of spiritual discipline as a mode of resistance is particularly useful for understanding the martial character of certain meditative practices; see my discussion toward the end of this chapter.

34. Peirce, *Collected Papers*, 5:533; see also 5:538.

35. Ibid., 5:538.

36. Saint Paul repeatedly emphasized the importance of self-control, and to a much greater degree in the spiritual life than in worldly pursuits. "Every athlete exercises self-control in all things," he observed in his first letter to the Corinthians (9:25). "They do it to receive a perishable wreath, but we an imperishable." He perceived it as a practical problem manifested in the gap between intentions and actions. "I do not understand my own actions" Paul announced as a prelude to one of his more famous confessions. "For I do not do what I want, but I do the very thing I hate. . . . I can will what is right, but I cannot do it. For I do not do the good that I want, but the evil I do not want is what I do: (Romans 7:15 and 18–19).

37. Examine Peirce's statement and interpretation of the "Law of Mind" in *Collected Papers*, 6:104 ff.

38. Ibid., 7:555.

39. Ibid., 5:295–98.

40. Consider Thich Nhat Hanh's proposals for transforming attitudes and perceptions by cultivating an awareness of the suffering of others: Nhat Hanh, *Love in Action: Writings on Nonviolent Social Change* (Berkeley, Calif.: Parallax Press, 1993), esp. chapters 5 through 10.

41. Consult Tu Wei-ming's brilliant essay "Confucianism" in *Our Religions,* ed. Arvind Sharma (San Francisco, Calif.: HarperCollins, 1993), pp. 141–227.

42. Peirce, *Collected Papers,* 5:493.

43. Peirce's critique of the "method of authority" appears in his problematic but famous essay "The Fixation of Belief"; ibid., 5:379–81.

44. In Peirce's "A Neglected Argument for the Reality of God"; ibid., 6:452–93; but see esp. 6:454 and 6:458–67.

45. Josiah Royce, *The Philosophy of Loyalty* (Nashville, Tenn.: Vanderbilt University Press, 1995), p. 35.

46. Ibid., p. 9.

47. Ibid., p. 21.

48. Ibid., p. 55.

49. Ibid., p. 56.

50. Ibid., p. 36.

51. Ibid., pp. 9, 74–76; see also Royce's *The Problem of Christianity* (Chicago, Ill.: University of Chicago Press, 1968), pp. 95–96 and 219–20.

52. Robert Neville characterized martial spirituality as primarily consisting in the purification of volition; see chapter 2 of his important early work *Soldier, Saint, Sage* (New York: Fordham University Press, 1978). In my estimation, this is still the finest treatment of that topic from a strictly philosophical perspective.

53. For a discussion of the complex interrelationship between abduction and induction in Peirce's theory of inquiry, see remarks in my *Boredom and the Religious Imagination,* pp. 144–48, 157–59, and my *Peirce's Philosophy of Religion,* p. 134 ff.

54. Van Ness develops this kind of a perspective on spiritual discipline (without emphasizing its martial character and while suppressing its theological significance) in chapter 7 of *Spirituality, Diversion, and Decadence.*

55. Peirce, *Collected Papers,* 6:228. Peirce wrote that "the movement of love is circular, at one and the same impulse projecting creations into independency and drawing them into harmony" (This would seem to be a particularly apt description from a philosopher's perspective of the kind of love that Ueshiba sought to embody in the flowing, circular movements of his aikidō.)

Postlude

1. Kristofer Schipper, *The Taoist Body*, trans. Karen C. Duval (Berkeley: University of California Press, 1993), pp. 9, 11, 62–63.

2. Dom Lorenzo Scupoli, *The Spiritual Combat, and a Treatise on Peace of Soul*, trans. William Lester and Robert Mohan (Rockford, Ill.: Tan Books, 1990), p. 197.

3. For a brilliant and influential account of the roots of violence in the self's "mimetic desire," examine Rene Girard's *Violence and the Sacred* (Baltimore, Md.: Johns Hopkins University Press, 1979), esp. chapter 6, p. 145 ff.

4. For two examples, consider Sulak Sivaraksa, *Seeds of Peace: A Buddhist Vision for Renewing Society* (Berkeley, Calif.: Parallax Press, 1992); and Thich Nhat Hanh, *Touching Peace: Practicing the Art of Mindful Living* (Berkeley, Calif.: Parallax Press, 1992).

5. Kisshomaru Ueshiba, *Spirit of Aikido* (Tokyo: Kodansha International, 1987), p. 102.

6. Schipper, *Taoist Body*, pp. 63, 141.

7. Charles S. Peirce, *Collected Papers of Charles Sanders Peirce*, ed. C. Hartshorne, P. Weiss, and A. Burks (Cambridge: Harvard University Press, 1935, 1958), 6:289.

8. Colossians, 3:14–15.

9. Scupoli, *Spiritual Combat*, p. 206.

10. *Lao Tsu: Tao Te Ching*, trans. Gia-Fu Feng and Jane English (New York: Vintage, 1997), chapter 50.

Index

STUDIES IN RELIGION & CULTURE